PORTALS
of
HEAVEN

REBECCA L. KING

DEDICATION

Bonita Gail Gaskins

Only God knows the countless hours, miles traveled and sleepless nights we have endured together to produce the materials to explain to others about the revelation of God's glory.

Never have I known anyone with the amount of knowledge you have concerning the Word of God. Your enthusiasm and encouragement has enhanced my encounters with God. I cherish your obedience to Him that has benefited all others for the kingdom.

CONTENTS

INTRODUCTION

Portals of Heaven is a book that God laid upon my heart to write in order for others to have the knowledge of open heavens. I experienced holy portals early on in my life and always knew that it was a gift that God had allowed me to experience so I could eventually share with others. There are heavenly blessings that God desires to pour forth upon the lives of His children but first we must have the knowledge of an open heaven in order for these blessings to come forth. Many people have experienced open portals before and simply did not know what to do with them and acted as if they never occurred to keep others from thinking that they were losing their minds. The more that I acknowledge holy portals of heaven, the more I experience holy portals of heaven.

God desires that we experience all that He has for us in this earthly realm but we first must realize that the things of God will not be normal. If you are looking for a normal book then I would suggest that you put this one down and search for another. Holy portals of heaven are supernatural and have the ability to change lives drastically for the good of those who love Him. You must humble yourself as you seek the supernatural knowledge of the open heavens and as you do, you will find the hidden mysteries of the kingdom of God.

This book pretty much speaks for itself and has the potential to cause a hunger within you that will take you into the signs, wonders and miracles of God. Don't be surprised when you begin to see things occur that are out of this world. Remember, God is omnipresent. He is everywhere at all times so therefore, He can do anything at anytime. God will allow you to see and hear things while reading this book that you never thought possible.

If you are ready to see and be more of God then sit back, read and revelate throughout the pages of this God-given book "Portals of Heaven."

Shalom,
Rebecca L. King

CHAPTER ONE

WHAT IS A PORTAL?

Webster's dictionary defines *'portal'* as a "doorway, gate, or entrance, especially a large and imposing one, any point or place of entry."

Then He said to him, I assure you, most solemnly I tell you all, you shall see heaven opened, and the angels of God ascending and descending upon the Son of Man!
John 1:51, AMP

What if you could see an open portal? Would you take the opportunity to look up and look in? The first open portal that I ever experienced was when I was eight years old. I was mowing my uncle's lawn when all of a sudden the clouds above me began to move away from each other like the parting of a sea. It was as if scrolls were on both sides of the heavenlies and eternity was being exposed. I was so frightened that I squinted my eyes as tight as I could and caught another gear on the lawn mower to try to outrun this bizarre happening. What was God trying to show me that day that I was too scared to handle? What has God shown you that you were to scared to handle? Little did I know that it would be thirty more years before I would experience this again.

OUR FEARS WILL KEEP US FROM SEEING INTO THE SUPERNATURAL.

Too many times, we squint our eyes shut and speed up to keep from supernaturally experiencing the things of God. Have you ever experienced the birth of a baby? This is the supernatural! Have you ever stopped on the side of the road just to savor the moment of a double rainbow? This, too, is supernatural. The supernatural experiences are intended for us to understand God more, not to scare us. It's the fear that is already within us that causes more fear. Repent of this fear and see God in the beautiful way that He desires for us (His creation) to see Him. We need to consider allowing God to manifest himself to us in His Own way for us to better understand Him. We have tried to keep God in a box long enough. We have been the ones inside the box, so why not open yourself up and see what God has in store for you? By the way, boxes are what we store the dead in. God cannot be dead, so let's just put the box up! May I lead you in a prayer?

Dear Heavenly Father,
I purpose and choose with my free will to repent for trying to keep you in a box of limitations and boundaries that would allow me to stay in control. I repent for the sin of fear that I have operated in as sin and ask You to forgive me, and I forgive myself. Please forgive me for all of the ways that I wouldn't let You express Yourself in my life in supernatural ways. I want to come out of the box so I can walk in the supernatural. In Jesus Name.

There hasn't been a lot of teaching on portals in the past simply because portals are supernatural. An open portal is an opening into the heavenlies. It is an open heaven. The closer we get to the second coming of Jesus Christ, the more natural the supernatural is going to become for those who have eyes to see and ears to hear. It should be natural for us to walk in the supernatural. The reason I have this teaching is because God gave me revelation on this subject matter, and He knew that I would teach it to other people as I received it from Him.

GOD'S EXPLANATION IS HIS REVELATION

Revelation is God's explanation of His original intentions. God desires to explain to us, His children, His kingdom intent for us here on earth as it is in heaven. Not only will God reveal to His children an explanation, He will reveal His original intentions. The explanation of His original intentions will inform your invalidations of their error. This is not a very popular teaching, but it is a powerful one. In this process, we have to be open to the good ways of God because we are accustomed to our brokenness. We must break our bad habits of calling evil good! We are so used to believing what man says rather than what God says that, when God speaks, we find what He says hard to believe. We, as human beings must get to the place where our obedience to God is more important than other people's approval. We must hear to see.

GOD'S ACCEPTANCE IS GREATER THAN MAN'S INFLUENCE.

Seven times in the second and third chapters of Revelation, the word of God speaks about having an ear to hear. When we hear the revelation of God we are able then to receive the promises of God. Every time the word says, "to those who hear," a promise is mentioned. I have underlined the promises for your attention.

"He who is able to hear, let him listen to and give heed to what the Spirit says to the assemblies (churches). To him

who overcomes (is victorious), <u>I will grant to eat [of the fruit] of the tree of life, which is in the paradise of God.</u>"

Revelation 2:7, AMP

"He who is able to hear, let him listen to and heed what the Spirit says to the assemblies (churches). He who overcomes (is victorious) <u>shall in no way be injured by the second death.</u>"

Revelation 2:11, AMP

"He who is able to hear, let him listen to and heed what the Spirit says to the assemblies (churches). To him who overcomes (conquers), <u>I will give to eat of the manna that is hidden, and I will give him a white stone with a new name engraved on the stone, which no one knows or understands except he who receives it.</u>"

Revelation 2:17, AMP

"And he who overcomes (is victorious) and who obeys My commands to the [very] end [doing the works that please Me], <u>I will give him authority and power over the nations; And he shall rule them with a sceptre (rod) of iron, as when earthen pots are broken in pieces, and [his power over them shall be] like that which I Myself have received from My Father; And I will give him the Morning Star.</u> He who is able to hear, let him listen to and heed what the [Holy] Spirit says to the assemblies (churches)."

Revelation 2:26-29, AMP

"<u>Thus shall he who conquers (is victorious) be clad in white garments, and I will not erase or blot out his name from the Book of Life; I will acknowledge him [as Mine] and I will confess his name openly before My Father and</u>

before His angels. He who is able to hear, let him listen to and heed what the [Holy] Spirit says to the assemblies (churches)."

Revelation 3:5-6, AMP

"He who overcomes (is victorious), I will make him a pillar in the sanctuary of My God; he shall never be put out of it or go out of it, and I will write on him the name of My God and the name of the city of My God, the new Jerusalem, which descends from My God out of heaven, and My own new name. He who can hear, let him listen to and heed what the Spirit says to the assemblies (churches)."

Revelation 3:12-13, AMP

"Behold, I stand at the door and knock; if anyone hears and listens to and heeds My voice and opens the door, I will come in to him and will eat with him, and he [will eat] with Me. He who overcomes (is victorious), I will grant him to sit beside Me on My throne, as I Myself overcame (was victorious) and sat down beside My Father on His throne."

Revelation 3:20-21, AMP

HEARING IS SEEING

Hearing is the most important thing that a Christian can do in this hour. If we hear, then we can overcome. In the natural, you see with your eyes and hear with your ears. However, in the supernatural you hear with your eyes and see with your heart. This is why it is so important to get your heart made whole so you can see whole-heartedly. When your heart is broken, then what you see is broken. We must get our hearts made whole so we can see the whole picture of God's plan. I prayed for years for God to fix my heart and

He finally told me that He couldn't. He said, "Every time that I fix it, you bring up the past and break it all over again." He continued to tell me that He would, however, give me a brand new heart. He also told me to guard and protect it because out of it flowed the issues of life.

> *"Keep and guard your heart with all vigilance and above all that you guard, for out of it flow the springs of life."*
> **Proverbs 4:23, AMP**

God allows my team and I to supernaturally pass out new hearts and the testimonies have been phenomenal!

Once you receive a brand new heart, you must guard it or you will allow it to be broken again. Be very careful not to break your own heart with self-bitterness, self-hatred, self-judgment, self-condemnation, false expectations of self, unforgiveness towards yourself, and all other issues that have to do with you being against you. Most autoimmune diseases stem from being against yourself. Would you like to receive a new heart right now? May we pray?

Dear Heavenly Father,
I purpose and choose with my free will to repent for any and all ways that I have participated in fear, rejection, and abandonment that have broken my precious heart. Forgive me, Lord, for breaking other people's hearts and for breaking my own. I ask that You take the old one out (place your hand over your broken heart) and give me a brand new one. Teach me to guard my new heart and flow in the greatest measure of intimacy that I have ever known. In Jesus' Name.

Having a broken heart means that you are a broken vessel. A broken vessel cannot carry the new wine of God's glory. Have you ever been to a good church service and felt spiritually full when you left? Unfortunately, the next day you felt emptier than the day before! This is because you have a cracked (broken) vessel that needs to be made whole so it can contain the new wine of God's glory. The night before, you were filled, but during the night you leaked out the very substance that God had filled you with. It is because your vessel was cracked. You're not the only one that this has happened to. Everybody has a crack!!! God desires us to be made whole so that we can contain His presence, which will give, both us and others, life. You can't give what you don't have.

If a portal is an opening or entryway, then we must be willing to open our minds and hearts to the understanding of the supernatural things of God if we are to see and hear supernaturally. The number one reason we close ourselves down is because of the fears and pains that have been caused by either ours or by other people's mistakes. False teachings have also created a sense of skepticism within us that cause us to miss out on the unseen things of God. There is a certain sense of fear that comes with opening your mind because of things that have been instilled within us that keep us from experiencing more of God. We somehow have fallen prey to the deception that, if we open our minds, something bad could come in.

I will give you an example: I called my grandfather one day and asked him if he would like to have lunch with one of my friends and I. He was seventy-five years old and stuck in his ways. He immediately said, *"No, I have been divorced for twenty-five years, and I am not interested in meeting your friend."* I said, *"Come on Papa, at least you will get a lunch out of the deal."* He agreed and met with us for lunch. I cleaned the kitchen afterwards and made a pot of coffee, and then I dismissed myself and allowed the two of them to become more acquainted. Three hours later, I returned as my grandfather was leaving, and I heard him tell my friend that he would see her again soon. He was a good bit older than she was. She was from a foreign country and was about to have to go back because of her visa. Her dream was to stay in the United States and become a citizen. He had been sick for ten years and had had his leg amputated which had left him disabled. They both were in need of a miracle. I told the two of them, *"Listen, Papa, you need a companion to help you, and she needs a husband for citizenship. Can't we be open-minded and see what God wants to do here?"* Three months later they were married, and they both were taken care of by God. They had to be open-minded for their miracles to come through. When we are open-minded we can live under an open heaven. Blessings come through an open heaven! When we are stuck in our ways, we can't walk in His ways. Again, God cannot be put in a box by any means, so if you're going to experience the supernatural you must look outside of the box. Live a little and you might find a whole lot! Who knows, you may stumble upon your healing as you seek Him in this unfamiliar place.

GOD IS ALWAYS FOUND
IN "UNFAMILIAR PLACES."

God doesn't make mistakes and it is no mistake that you are reading this book. God desires to take you into a place that has no limitations or false expectations. He wants to take you into the supernatural realm of His Presence (the unseen realm), the Glory Realm. I believe that in this supernatural hour God desires to show us the unseen things of His heavenly realm while we remain here on earth. There are things that God has for us, but our closed-mindedness has to be opened in order for God to allow His blessings to come forth through our portals. I guess you could say that God wants to show His kingdom off here a little bit before His kingdom truly descends. In all actuality we, His people, are supposed to be pulling heaven down to earth by way of our faith. We achieve this by using our portal as a place of transportation for the eternal to invade the earthly. God needs the visible to call forth the invisible. Are you available?

"Now faith is the substance of things hoped for, the evidence of things not seen."

Hebrews 11:1, KJV

The revelation on this scripture is: *faith* is the substance *hoped* for, the *evidence* of the *unseen*!!! The evidence of the unseen? We have used this scripture for years to convince ourselves that things that are not seen can be hoped for. Well, how about trying this on for size? God has to have a substance (your mind) in order for hope to occur. This hope is in a God that you have never seen before, which causes a shift in the supernatural that brings forth the evidence of the unseen. Therefore, you begin to see between the barrier that the fall of man and sin created and the original intentions of our Creator (the unseen realm). Don't make this hard: Just believe and go with the flow and you will be amazed at what God allows you to experience. We so many times think that if it isn't hard then it isn't God. We are so accustomed to hardships, that we associate serving God with complications. For example: We boil tea to make it hot and then put ice in it to make it cold (and if that were not enough), then put sugar in it to make it sweet, then lemon to make it sour (then try to relax while drinking it)!!!

HOW'S THAT WORKING FOR YOU?

We normally use **Hebrews 11:1** to hope for things that we do not yet have, when in all actuality the **substance** in this passage of scripture has to do with our **mind**. When Jesus turned the water into wine in (**John 2**), the substance was the **water**. He had to use a **"tangible substance"** as an example of our mind. Water was the substance; wine was the miracle. You must have a substance in order to have a miracle. In other words, your substance is your mind offered openly to see and hear the supernatural before the supernatural can come forth. You must give faith permission to be larger than your mind. Have you ever tried to explain something to somebody and they just didn't get it? You may have used the old saying, "never mind." **Never-mindedness is excusing the mind from understanding that which could bring forth the supernatural.** When we don't see God move (or He takes too long), we go into the "never mind mentality", when it is our mind that He needs to use as the water before the wine. Be very careful not to "never mind" the wine!

**NEVER MINDEDNESS IS EVIDENCE
OF DOUBLE MINDEDNESS!**

Portals have a lot to do with our minds and hearts, as you will see later in this book. Portals can, however, be seen by the natural eyes. The photo on the front of this book shows portals coming out of the heavenlies invading the earth. The shafts of light are either vertical or diagonal shaped tunnels of eternal illumination expressing themselves upon the earth realm as God's people acknowledge Him in all of His glory. You may have seen these portals before and sensed something different about them or even been captivated by their beauty. As you acknowledge His glory and then wait for God's explanation of these manifestations, He will take you into an open portal. However, the lack of knowing exactly what portals are will hinder you from acknowledging God's glory for further revelation of the unseen. The mind that operates in fear, doubt, and unbelief, however, will justify these eternal manifestations as "just openings in the clouds with the sun shining through." The next time you see a rainbow, stop long enough to acknowledge its beauty, and then ask God to give you revelation on its intentions. You will be amazed at what He will have to say. God is trying to show His creation signs in the heavenlies and all we must do is look and be willing to hear.

You have to have an open mind
to see an open portal.

"For now we see through a glass, darkly; but then face to face: now I know in part; but then shall I know even as also I am known."

1 Corinthians 13:12, KJV

When you have a face-to-face encounter with God and His revelation sets you free, then the guilt and shame that you have allowed to torment you all of these years has to stop. Your God doesn't hold it against you, nor does your baby. Therefore, you must not hold it against yourself any longer. Don't get me wrong; I do not support abortion! My adopted son was supposed to be aborted and God intervened. I do, however, support the brokenhearted who have participated in past abortions and need help finding their healing. May I lead you in a prayer?

Dear Heavenly Father,
I purpose and choose with my free will to repent for any and all ways that I participated in abortion. I also repent for any un-forgiveness that I have held towards myself for my responsibility in abortion (and/or abortions). Lord, I ask that You forgive me, and I forgive myself. I also repent for the guilt and shame that I have allowed to operate in my life as sin. I cancel this debt in Jesus' name. Holy Spirit, please heal my broken heart and speak Your words of truth.

When we entered into this earth realm, our portal delivered us here. Remember, a portal is an entrance into the earth realm that originates at the throne of God. A portal is an open heaven! Portals remain open as we walk throughout life to transfer eternal annuities into the earth realm. Scriptural evidence of open portals is important because we need to see this in the Word. How can we be seated in heavenly places right now?

> *"And hath raised us up together, and made us sit together in heavenly places in Christ Jesus:"*
>
> **Ephesians 2:6, KJV**

How can we be seated in heaven and be here on earth at the same time? Through our open portal. The more you realize that you live under an open portal, the more access to heaven you have. The open portal begins at the throne of God; so anytime you need heaven to invade earth, just use your open portal as the access. The promises of God also travel through your portal to come into this earthly existence. Signs, wonders and miracles also travel through your open portal. The reason not many people are experiencing these signs, wonders and miracles is simply because they have no knowledge of the access that we have to eternity through our open portals.

I would like to give you an example of open access to heaven by way of a portal. I had a phone call one afternoon concerning a little boy who had been accidentally shot in the chest. I instantly went into my open portal to the throne of God and requested that the little boy receive new lungs, heart, arteries, blood vessels, muscle tissue and anything else that he needed for his recovery. He was flown to a larger hospital and by the time he arrived, his lungs were healed. He only stayed in the hospital for three days after the gunshot wound to his chest. To God be all the GLORY! I actually saw the new lungs coming down from heaven as we accessed the throne of God.

There is a geographical location of a known open portal at Moravian Falls, North Carolina. I visited this place not too long ago and was impressed with the atmospheric impression of eternity. It was nice to go to a place and sit under an open heaven, which I believe is an ancient open portal. Ancient open portal means it has been there for many generations, and it is still expanding because people travel from all over the world to this little place to experience a miraculous manifestation of God's presence. The peoples' expectations and expressions expand this atmosphere as they watch in amazement as the eternal invades the earth. We went to another location that was dedicated to prayer, which just happened to be on top of a mountain. We prayed with some people there, and the glory and revelation of God was extraordinary. Once the people that we prayed with descended the mountain, they passed a few young men on their way to the top of the mountain. We were about to leave when suddenly one of the young men called out to us and said, "Hey are y'all from Georgia?" We said, "Well, yes we are." He said, "We just passed some people who said that we needed to get up here quick and receive prayer from you ladies."

We agreed with the young men and started praying for God to reveal Himself. After prayer, one of the young men asked me, "Have you all seen an open portal up here?" I immediately testified of our experience and then went on to explain to him that what he carried was also an open portal. He looked at me like I had two heads and said, "What do you mean I carry an open portal?" Why was it so hard for him to believe that he could be carrying an open portal? I asked him if it would be all right if I took a picture of him and showed him his portal. He was shocked by my request but agreed. Quickly, I grabbed my camera and snapped a shot. He was amazed at what he saw! He was standing in the middle of a huge circle of colors that were the colors of the rainbow. His buddy was really impressed with this supernatural manifestation and innocently asked if he had an open portal, too? I said, "Of course you do," and I took a picture of him as well. Again, an open portal was surrounding another one of God's kids.

COLORS OF THE RAINBOW

I remember the first time that a rainbow ever manifested around me like a carousel of colors. Open portals allow the rainbow of

God (His promises) to manifest in your presence. I was amazed by the manifestation of God's promises coming to me. God told me that the revelation behind the manifestation was that "religion had people chasing treasures at the end of the rainbow." Have you ever chased a rainbow because you had been told your whole life that there was a treasure at the end of it?

> *"I do set my bow in the cloud, and it shall be for a token of a covenant between me and the earth. And it shall come to pass, when I bring a cloud over the earth, that the bow shall be seen in the cloud: And I will remember my covenant, which is between me and you and every living creature of all flesh; and the waters shall no more become a flood to destroy all flesh. And the bow shall be in the cloud; and I will look upon it, that I may remember the everlasting covenant between God and every living creature of all flesh that is upon the earth."*
>
> **Genesis 9:13-16, KJV**

Notice here that the Lord continuously mentions that the bow will be in the cloud. The cloud is God's glory that He demonstrates His promise in, simply because God cannot look upon sin.

> *"Thou art of purer eyes than to behold evil, and canst not look on iniquity: wherefore lookest thou upon them that deal treacherously, and holdest thy tongue when the wicked devoureth the man that is more righteous than he?"*
>
> **Habakkuk 1:13, KJV**

God places the cloud of His glory upon His people to cover us so that His presence can go with us wherever we go. Jesus' blood that was shed on Calvary made it possible to go beyond the veil in the temple into the holy of holies. When the veil was rent, the glory of God was able to come forth from behind the veil because Jesus made the ultimate sacrifice for the sin of mankind. In other words, the glory cloud of God was no longer veiled in the presence of God's people. The cloud of God's glory could now come forth to cover His people once again as it had done before with the Israelites. The glory of God was behind the veil because Moses had covered the glory of God with a veil.

> *"And the children of Israel saw the face of Moses, that the skin of Moses' face shone: and Moses put the veil upon his face again, until he went in to speak with him."*
> **Exodus 34:35, KJV**

Because of sin in our lives, God still has to cover us with His glory because He cannot look upon sin. He places the glory cloud between us so that He can go with us wherever we dwell. The glory of God (which is the unexplained, convincing manifestation of God) was beyond the veil but now is unveiled so that we can be covered. This is not unusual behavior for God because He placed the same cloud of His presence over the Israelites as they exited Egypt.

> *"And the Lord went before them by day in a pillar of a cloud, to lead them the way; and by night in a pillar of fire, to give them light; to go by day and night:"*
> **Exodus 13:21, KJV**

The glory of God was beyond the veil but now, because of the blood of Jesus, the veil is taken away and the glory cloud of God is resting upon His people. The evidence of the glory of God resting upon you and covering you is the amount of rest you are walking in. Once the veil was rent, mankind had access to remove the veil that had been upon their face keeping them from seeing the face of God. The rainbow is symbolic of the promises of God, and when we acknowledge His glory, His promises come to us. The first day that the rainbow manifested around me, God told me that, "I no longer had to chase anything, because He had manifested His glory upon me, and I was now the treasure." God's glory is chasing you! When you can see yourself as the treasure, you no longer have to chase after the promises of God; His promises come to you. We chase after things in life only to realize in the end that we have been like a dog chasing his own tail!

WHEN THE VEIL IS RENT,
THE RAINBOW IS SENT.

CHAPTER 2

UNVEILING THE BRIDE

God desires to unveil us like He unveiled the holy of holies. The word *'unveil' means* to reveal oneself. God rent the veil for us so that we could be revealed to Him and all of His glory. This process is not a stripping away like religion would have us think; it is more of an intimate moment when the groom removes the bride's veil. So many times when things don't go right in our lives, we think that God is stripping us to make His points. God has never stripped me of anything, but He has intimately revealed things to me to remove me from situations that would eventually cause me harm. If you feel as if God has stripped you to show you things, how's that working for you? Would you like to be free from the torment that has kept you from entering into the holy of holies?

Dear Heavenly Father,
I purpose and choose with my free will to repent for any and all ways that I have held bitterness and unforgiveness towards You because I thought that You had stripped me to show me Your way. Father, forgive me for allowing religion to ruin our relationship. Help me to understand that the enemy wants me to feel stripped so I will continue to try to hide my sin, guilt and shame. Lord, I desire to stand before You as naked in Your sight

that I may be revealed unto myself and to You. I cancel this debt
of clothing myself with the counterfeit garments of the adversary's
accusations and desire to be free from me. In Jesus name.

To God, we are the Holy of Holies. We are the meeting place
that He desires to dwell within. In taking a step further, we are the
temple.

"Know ye not that ye are the temple of God, and that the
Spirit of God dwelleth in you?"
                                  1 Corinthians 3:16, 6:19, KJV

God wants to fill you, the temple of Himself, with who He is,
which is His glory.

"And the temple was filled with smoke from the glory of
God, and from his power; and no man was able to enter
into the temple, till the seven plagues of the seven angels
were fulfilled."
                                           Revelation 15:8, KJV

The word of God is the instruction for life that eternity has made
available. The veil was rent in the temple, so it must be rent in us as
well. For we are the "Well of God's Glory Unveiled"! You can read
more about how to become the well of God's glory in my first book,
"The Well of God's Glory Unveiled." I also have a 5 disc audio
CD teaching on **"How to Unveil the Glory in My Life"**, which is
a great tool for discovering your destiny.

The veil also represents layers of counterfeit clothing that we have
covered ourselves with to conceal the guilt and shame of our past
and present sins. Remember, sin will keep you separated from the
presence of God. It was handed down to us dishonestly when Adam
and Eve hid behind a bush with fig leaves as their false covering. We

must remove all coverings that are not of God. God is our ultimate covering (Isaiah 58:8)!

> *"Neither is there any creature that is not manifest in his sight: but all things are naked and opened unto the eyes of him with whom we have to do."*
>
> **Hebrews 4:13, KJV**

God asked Adam, *"Who told you that you were naked?"* It was not God's original intention for us to be covered with anything but His presence. In other words, who told you how to cover up with something else besides My presence? Ever since the fall of man (which has been our whole life), we have automatically covered up with false garments of the enemy's accusations so that God and others couldn't see our nakedness. Man chose to cover himself with the finest fabrics (fabrication) of satan's wardrobe (robe of war), which was the counterfeit covering. Ever since then, we have been trying to clothe ourselves with garments in life that never correctly fit us because we were tailor-made to carry His glory. Does this make sense? We are always trying to find things in life that fit! The garments of His glory are peace, hope and love. It is time for us to clean out our closets, get rid of those false garments, and clothe ourselves with the true presence of His glory.

There remains a veil upon the minds and hearts of God's people even now as the word is read concerning the glory of God. The veil was rent so that we could rest in His presence. God desires for us to dwell in His presence. Why rent when you can own? You can't rest until the veil is rent.

> *"For if that which is done away was glorious, much more that which remaineth is glorious. Seeing then that we have such hope, we use great plainness of speech: And not as Moses, which put a veil over his face, that the children of*

Israel could not steadfastly look to the end of that which is abolished: But their minds were blinded: for until this day remaineth the same veil untaken away in the reading of the old testament; which veil is done away in Christ. But even unto this day, when Moses is read, the veil is upon their heart. Nevertheless when it shall turn to the Lord, the veil shall be taken away. Now the Lord is that Spirit: and where the Spirit of the Lord is, there is liberty. But we all, with open face beholding as in a glass the glory of the Lord, are changed into the same image from glory to glory, even as by the Spirit of the Lord."

2 Corinthians 3:11-18, KJV

Another revelation that God gave me concerning Moses veiling himself was that he stuttered.

"But Moses said to the Lord, Behold, I am of deficient and impeded speech; how then shall Pharaoh listen to me?"

Exodus 6:30, AMP

Notice here in the scripture above that it says, "we use plainness of speech." Speech problems usually have something to do with childhood traumas, and Moses certainly had his share of traumas. Could it be that Moses was insecure when it came to his being a voice for God, and he veiled himself because of the way that he felt about his flaws?

Be very careful not to veil what God places upon you simply because of your own insecurities. God can use your weakness as His very own strength.

HE IS OUR STRENGTH!

"And he said unto me, My grace is sufficient for thee: for my strength is made perfect in weakness. Most gladly therefore will I rather glory in my infirmities, that the power of Christ may rest upon me."

2 Corinthians 12:9, KJV

We tend to hide our weaknesses so other people will not realize that we are weak. Don't let your insecurities keep you from being a voice for God.

Dear Heavenly Father,

I purpose and choose with my free will to repent for any and all ways that I have allowed my insecurities to veil the glory of Your presence that You have placed upon my life. Lord, fill every hole of invalidation within me that enables insecurities to abide. Forgive me for all of the ways that I have allowed my insecurities to rule and reign in my life when I should have allowed You to. I cancel this debt in Jesus' name.

I had a visit one day from a drug dealer who wanted to get saved. He came to my house and said, *"Mmmms. Beeeeecckkky, I-I-I wwwwaaaat tttooo bbbbbbee sssaaaavvvved."* I said, *"Praise God,"* and then I led him in the prayer of salvation. He, too, was like Moses and had a speech impediment. I asked him about his relationship with his daddy and he explained to me that he had never known his dad. I asked him if I could pray a trauma prayer with him about never knowing his dad and instantly when we said, "amen," he no longer stuttered. That was 5 years ago and both he and his family are currently doing great. To God be the glory!

STEADY NOT STUTTER.

If we would rend the veil in our own lives, we could live under the glory cloud of God and have access to His presence at all times through an open portal. The blood of Jesus allows the glory cloud to cover us both day and night that we might be free from anything that would otherwise kill us in the holy presence of God. Moses had to be covered as he was learning about the glory of God. God covered him as He passed by him in the cleft of the rock.

> *"And it shall come to pass, while my glory passeth by, that I will put thee in a cleft of the rock, and will cover thee with my hand while I pass by:"*
> **Exodus 33:22, KJV**

As he learned more about the glory, he was eventually covered in the glory to the point that his face shone like the heavenlies. It scared the people around him because the glory was too much for their sins. Sins do keep us separated from God, but if we will go past our sins and on into the glory, then the glory will get us over our sin. Don't back off from God because of your sin, but pursue God in the midst of your sin that He may set you free. Moses was a sinful man just like you and me, but that didn't keep him from carrying the glory of God.

The contentious people that Moses was called to lead kept him from carrying the glory. He allowed himself to be entangled in the emotions of other people. A normal day at the office for Moses was a desk full of complaints that consisted of people being too cold or too hot, too hungry or too thirsty, too sad or too mad. His work piled up on Him, and He became overloaded with what I call **false burden bearing**. False burden bearing is when you take on the load of other people's problems because you feel as if you are expected to. A good indication that you operate under false burden bearing is if you complain about having to do the very things that you are expected to do. You do not have the right to complain about the things that you tolerate.

The thing about Moses' false burden bearing was the fact that it was going to eventually keep him out of his destiny. Don't let the false expectations of others keep you from walking in your destiny. After the death of Moses, Joshua moved on the scene as commander in chief. Joshua operated under an open portal and took the promised land within days. Don't get me wrong, Moses operated under an open heaven as well, but he allowed the influence of negative emotions of others to constrict his portal. The Israelites that were used to complaining to Moses that they were thirsty also complained to Joshua. However, when Joshua (being under an open portal) was asked to get them something to drink he said, **"Dig your own well."** Open portals will take you into places in your life that you have never been able to conquer and then allow you to abide in those once impossible places. By the way, false burden bearing is the reason we carry a multitude of unnecessary back, neck and shoulder pain that can subside as a result of a little repentance. May I lead you in a prayer?

FALSE BURDEN BEARING
CONSTRICTS YOUR PORTAL.

Dear Heavenly Father,
I purpose and choose with my free will to repent for any and all fear, rejection and abandonment that I have operated in as sin. I ask You to forgive me, and I forgive myself for all of the ways that I have participated in false burden bearing. I also forgive the people who have expected me to take care of their needs unnecessarily thus keeping me from my destiny. I forgive all others for teaching me that I was always supposed to do for others even when I did not do for myself. I also ask You to forgive me for finding validation in always doing for others because I thought that I was not worthy to be done for. I cancel this debt, in Jesus' name.

CONVERTING THE SEA INTO THEE

"For all have sinned, and come short of the glory of God."
Romans 3:23, KJV

God's glory is His presence, and He wants to saturate you and your sin with His love. The more that you learn about the glory of God, the more God fills you with the glory. The more that you acknowledge the glory of God, the greater the glory becomes in your life. It is not unusual for me to acknowledge the glory in every conversation that I have; therefore, it is not unusual that the manifested glory is so prevalent in my life. The more glory that you desire, the more glory you have to give.

"For the earth shall be filled with the knowledge of the glory of the Lord, as the waters cover the sea."
Habakkuk 2:14, KJV

The earth in this passage of scripture refers to us, His earthen vessels. He desires to fill us as the waters cover the sea. That's Deep!

LET IT RAIN.

LET IT RAIN

It was the summer of '89 when I attended my senior trip in Panama City, Florida. I knew the call of God that was on my life but I really wanted to live a little before submitting myself unto the Lord. God would not leave me alone so I hollered up into the heavenlies, "God, if you want me so bad then let it rain for seven days straight". What was I thinking? This was my senior trip, first free week from parents, rules and all restrictions. It started raining and it rained seven days and seven nights straight. It was still another ten years before I submitted my life to Christ, but that senior trip was always in the back of my mind. Twenty-four years later, I was invited to preach a conference in Panama City and the name of the conference was "LET IT RAIN".

While at the conference, I decided to take a swim in the Gulf of Mexico before one of my meetings. My team accompanied me and we entered the refreshing waters of God's glory. Water represents the glory of God. There was a sense of excitement and mischief, as we knew that the meeting time was approaching quickly. It was almost as if we desired to be in His glory more than we desired to be in the presence of many others. This happens a lot, as the eternal impression of God saturates your very being. As we jumped over each wave anticipating the arrival of the next, I felt God urging me to go under and open my eyes. I was stunned at His request, but I promptly obeyed Him and went under the water with my eyes wide open. To my surprise, I was able to see without any burning sensation. I immediately came up out of the water and testified of this miraculous manifestation. I encouraged my team to try this to see what their experience would be, and the same thing happened to them. I took it a step further, as I scooped up a handful of water and put it to my mouth for a drink, to my surprise again, it was fresh water. I need to remind you here that the Gulf of Mexico is salt water.

God gave me the revelation of this extraordinary excursion simply because He desires that we exercise eternity here on earth. God's Word reveals in Revelation that:

"And I saw a new heaven and a new earth: for the first heaven and the first earth were passed away; and there was no more sea."

Revelations 21:1, KJV

I then realized that there will be no sea in heaven simply because we will be the sea! Do you SEE what I'm saying? When we are able to see like Him, there will be no more need for the SEA. God revealed to me that the only reason there is a sea is because the earth had to have a supernatural reservoir reserved to contain the revelation of God until His creation could be filled with the knowledge of the glory of the Lord.

"But [the time is coming when] the earth shall be filled with the knowledge of the glory of the Lord as the waters cover the sea."

Habakkuk 2:14, AMP

More confirmation of this is that the sea will also contain salt until creation can swallow the revelation that we are the salt of the earth. The sea holds the salt until creation becomes the salt of the earth. When we receive the revelation that we are greater than the element water, then we can be filled with the flavor of God.

DO YOU SEE THE SEA IN ME?

God desires that we go to the depths of who He is and seek out the hidden places of His revelation.

"Deep calleth unto deep at the noise of thy waterspouts: all thy waves and thy billows are gone over me."

Psalms 42:7, KJV

God is calling forth a remnant to go deep, no matter what the price. If you dive into revelation, you will get wet. It never made sense to me why some people go swimming and try not to get their hair wet. You can't dive in and not get your head wet. It is your head (mind) that needs to be submerged in the revelation of God's glory so you can begin to have His thoughts instead of your own.

No wonder people still hesitate to go deep with God into the holy of holies. When the priest would enter into the holy of holies in the old testament, he would tie bells around his ankles, and if the bells stopped ringing the other priests would know to pull his dead body back out.

> *"A gold bell and a pomegranate, a gold bell and a pomegranate, round about on the skirts of the robe. Aaron shall wear the robe when he ministers, and its sound shall be heard when he goes [alone] into the Holy of Holies before the Lord and when he comes out, lest he die there."*
>
> **Exodus 28:34-35, AMP**

In other words, when you carry the glory of God, you have to get over yourself. The process of getting over yourself will heal you and not kill you. The priests prepared themselves for one day in His presence. Is it coincidental that we go to church one day a week, when we are supposed to be the church? Once a year, the priest would go into the holy of holies, and he would prepare all year for that one day. God desires that we live in His presence everyday, not just on certain days of the year.

> *"One day in His glorious presence is better than 1000 years anywhere else."*
>
> **Psalms 84:10, (paraphrase)**

If we would learn more about God's glory and walk in His covering, then as His presence comes in His glory would drive out our sin. When sin is driven out, sickness has to go as well. The glory of God fills all of the empty holes within us. Emptiness provides easy access for afflictions. Emptiness is evidence of the lack of the presence of God. Emptiness is evidence of no intimacy! Sometimes we sin because we have a need to be filled and have no knowledge of the glorious access that heaven has made available. The glory of God desires to fill you so you have no need to be fulfilled by other people or things.

HIS GLORY WILL DRIVE OUT YOUR SIN AS HIS PRESENCE COMES IN.

I like the way Ezekiel explained seeing the glory. By the way, this happened through his portal:

> *"Like the appearance of the bow that is in the cloud on the day of rain, so was the appearance of the brightness round about. This was the appearance of the likeness of the glory of the Lord. And when I saw it, I fell upon my face and I heard a voice of One speaking."*
>
> **Ezekiel 1:28, AMP**

The glorious thing about seeing the glory is that you automatically hear the voice of the One speaking. In the natural, you hear with your ears and see with your eyes. However, in the supernatural you hear with your eyes and see with your heart. That is why you must get over yourself and get your heart healed so you can see whole-heartedly. Notice that God manifested Himself to Ezekiel in the rainbow! This was the first experience that Ezekiel had with the glory of God. Take note that it was again in the cloud! This is glorious! He described it as a rainbow appearing around the throne of God. He was actually in a portal that allowed him to see into the heavenlies and hear the revelations of God.

HEAR WITH YOUR EYES AND SEE WITH YOUR HEART.

When you allow yourself to believe instead of achieve, then you, too, can visit heaven through an open portal. It is more important to God that His children believe instead of achieve. There is nothing you can do to make this happen; just believe that it can happen, and it will happen.

One of the first examples of an open portal that I noticed was when God told John to "come up here."

"After this I looked, and behold, a door standing open in heaven! And the first voice which I had heard addressing me like [the calling of] a war trumpet said, Come up here, and I will show you what must take place in the future."
Revelation 4:1, AMP

May I add here that John, too, experienced the glory of God in the colors of the rainbow?

"Then I saw another mighty angel coming down from heaven, robed in a cloud, with a [halo like a] rainbow over his head; his face was like the sun, and his feet (legs) were like columns of fire."
Revelation 10:1, AMP

God took John up into his portal and showed him things that would take place in the future. Why is it so hard to believe that God took John up, but He won't take us up?

Again, we see that the glory comes in the cloud! Usually, when I testify of a rainbow experience, it manifests in the presence of the ones listening. Be on the lookout for a rainbow manifesting in your presence, and you, too, will experience this phenomenon. I have a booklet called, **"Clouds of Confusion"**, that can help you to understand how the cloud of confusion comes as the counterfeit before His glory is manifested. The enemy will send a cloud of confusion to distract you from what God has for you. If you have been under a cloud or fog of confusion, will you join me in this prayer?

> *Dear Heavenly Father,*
> *I purpose and choose with my free will to repent of any and all confusion that I have walked in that has kept me from walking under the cloud of your glory. You are not the author of confusion. You are the author of PEACE. Please forgive me for participating in confusion, and I forgive all others who have brought confusion into my life. I cancel this cloud of confusion and call forth the cloud of Your glory to guide, protect, and hide me for the rest of my life. In Jesus' name.*

I was invited to speak at a national conference once, and all the other speakers were much more seasoned than I. Just because you have been saved for seventy-five years doesn't mean that you have all of God that you need. There were five different speakers in different rooms, and you could choose which class you wanted to participate in. I was the new kid on the block, so I didn't have many participants. The Bible says:

> **"For where two or three are gathered together in my name, there am I in the midst of them."**
>
> **Matthew 18:20, KJV**

It doesn't matter how many people there are because God is still the main one. Before I started class, an elderly man walked up to me and asked me about what information I had to offer him? I looked at him and said, "If you really want to know, come on in." He sat through my whole class and I spoke about the rainbow manifesting in my presence. I wasn't real sure how much this old guy was soaking up because he seemed a bit religious at the start. He was an older mature Christian who was set in his ways. However, after the service, he began to cry, and he told me of the manifestation of the rainbow that had followed him on his recent trip home. He told me that he asked God to tell him what it meant and weeks later he found himself sitting in my class hearing the testimony of the rainbow manifestation that brings you into the revelation that you are the treasure. He realized that day that he was the treasure and that the rainbow was chasing him. This is what I call an open portal. It was so funny because after the class he brought his buddies over to my table and began to tell them about the revelations and manifestations in our ministry. Unfortunately, his buddies acted just like he did before he came to my class.

I'm reminded of another time when some people came to stay at my home because they wanted to experience the supernatural. They had been there for several days and seemed a little discouraged because they had not seen anything manifest. We were riding down the road and suddenly a portal opened in the heavenlies, and I called it to their attention. The portal was a round hole in the heavenlies that was filled with the colors of the rainbow. They began to acknowledge it and praise God for allowing them to partake in such an incredible eternal experience. They desired to see more. Acknowledgment is an opportunity for an individual to experience eternity. We must first acknowledge the glory of God, and as we do so, the glory comes forth.

ACKNOWLEDGING THE GLORY IS AN ACT OF FAITH THAT CONSISTS OF EXPECTATION OF AN ETERNAL EXPERIENCE.

I prayed, "God let them see something that they have never seen before." Suddenly, there was an astronomical upside-down rainbow that appeared in the heavenlies. Glory to God! They were shocked that God would do this for them. We took pictures of this awesome event and continued to praise the Lord throughout the afternoon.

God gave me magnificent revelation of this manifestation. When we are willing to see as He sees, then He can reveal to us His original intentions. In other words, everything since the fall of man has been turned upside down from what God originally intended. When we look into an open portal, things are seen the way God intended for them to be seen. To us, here in this fallen state, the rainbow is in the shape of a frown, but to God from where He sits, it is a smile. God desires to turn our weeping into joy by showing us His glory that comes through our open portals. Since then, God has allowed me to see a double upside-down rainbow. Nothing like a double smile from God! To God be the GLORY.

INTIMACY UNVEILS UNDERSTANDING

Now that you are learning more about portals, you will be able to acknowledge God in all of His glory, and God will allow you to go into the unseen places of His presence that few people know of. Intimacy is the access to eternity. Love is the greatest gift.

"And so faith, hope, love abide [faith—conviction and belief respecting man's relation to God and divine things; hope—joyful and confident expectation of eternal salvation; love—true affection for God and man, growing out of God's love for and in us], these three; but the greatest of these is love."

1 Corinthians 13:13, AMP

As you walk in love, in return, the love of God brings forth understanding. In other words, the love that you walk in is the example of acknowledging the love of God, and when love is acknowledged it has to become greater. When you love someone, you try harder to understand his/her ways. Your love for them, when acknowledged, will bring forth a manifestation of a greater observation of understanding. God loves us so much that He gave His only be-gotten Son for us even though we were yet sinners. Love covers a multitude of sins; so as we love one another, let's try harder to understand each other.

TRUE LOVE IS THE WISDOM OF GOD.

There are two ingredients that you must have in order to walk in the wisdom of God: knowledge and understanding.

> *"And he changeth the times and the seasons: he removeth kings, and setteth up kings: he giveth wisdom unto the wise, and <u>knowledge</u> to them that know <u>understanding</u>:"*
> **Daniel 2:21, KJV**

Knowledge and understanding must be acquired before op-erating in the **WISDOM** of God. One without the other could be devastating to others. Many religious people have knowledge without understanding. Knowledge without understanding is like love without compassion. You have to have compassion to have love! Compassion is the compass that leads us to passion. The evi-dence of lack of compassion is dread instead of desire. I'm sure the soldiers who crucified Christ had loved ones in their lives, but they did not have compassion for the One who loved the whole world.

One without the other causes confusion and misunderstanding of intimacy. The soldiers did not have the wisdom of God until they had understanding added to their knowledge which brought forth the revelation of love. The wisdom of God revealed to the soldiers that truly this was the Son of God. Understanding is the revelation that comes when one understands what God is saying. God loves us so much that He desires for us to understand Him. Revelation is every word that proceeds out of the mouth of God. Jesus was talking about this on the Mount of Temptation.

"Wisdom is the principal thing; therefore get wisdom: and with all thy getting get understanding."

Proverbs 4:7, KJV

If wisdom is the principal, then we must be the prudent student of understanding.

Dear Heavenly Father,
I purpose and choose with my free will to repent for all the ways that I have leaned unto my own understanding which has kept me from receiving Your wisdom. Forgive me for all of the ways that I trusted in my own understanding, which was formed from the experiences of my past situations instead of Your eternal direction for my life. Teach me Your ways that I may receive a heart of wisdom. In Jesus' name.

Some people call this intimate place **"The Secret Place,"** but I call it a place of TRUE INTIMACY (In-to-me-u-c)! When we abide in this place of intimacy, we abide under the shelter of the Almighty.

"He who dwells in the secret place of the Most High shall remain stable and fixed under the shadow of the Almighty [Whose power no foe can withstand]. I will say of the Lord, He is my Refuge and my Fortress, my God; on Him I lean and rely, and in Him I [confidently] trust! For [then] He will deliver you from the snare of the fowler and from the deadly pestilence. [Then] He will cover you with His pinions, and under His wings shall you trust and find refuge; His truth and His faithfulness are a shield and a buckler. You shall not be afraid of the terror of the night, nor of the arrow (the evil plots and slanders of the wicked) that flies by day, Nor of the pestilence that stalks in darkness, nor

of the destruction and sudden death that surprise and lay waste at noonday. A thousand may fall at your side, and ten thousand at your right hand, but it shall not come near you. Only a spectator shall you be [yourself inaccessible in the secret place of the Most High] as you witness the reward of the wicked. Because you have made the Lord your refuge, and the Most High your dwelling place, There shall no evil befall you, nor any plague or calamity come near your tent. For He will give His angels [especial] charge over you to accompany and defend and preserve you in all your ways [of obedience and service]. They shall bear you up on their hands, lest you dash your foot against a stone. You shall tread upon the lion and adder; the young lion and the serpent shall you trample underfoot. Because he has set his love upon Me, therefore will I deliver him; I will set him on high, because he knows and understands My name [has a personal knowledge of My mercy, love, and kindness—trusts and relies on Me, knowing I will never forsake him, no, never]. He shall call upon Me, and I will answer him; I will be with him in trouble, I will deliver him and honor him. With long life will I satisfy him and show him My salvation."

Psalms 91, AMP

In order to dwell in this secret place, you must be able to trust in Him with your whole heart and not just half-heartedly. Remember, God is unveiling His bride. If you are the bride then you must love the bridegroom with all of your heart. It is in the secret place, the holy of holies, where He meets with us intimately and removes the veil that has kept us from being revealed. God desires to allow His people to see Him in all of His glory here, but few people do, because of lack of knowledge.

THE LACK OF KNOWLEDGE WILL
KEEP YOU FROM THE SECRET PLACE.

Acknowledgment is the action of knowledge. In order to acknowledge God's glory, you must know His glory. How many people have ended up in divorce because they married the groom without knowing him? You must know to be able to acknowledge and that will keep you from being divorced and destroyed.

"My people are destroyed for lack of knowledge: because thou hast rejected knowledge, I will also reject thee, that thou shalt be no priest to me: seeing thou hast forgotten the law of thy God, I will also forget thy children."

Hosea 4:6, KJV

HERE NOT OVER YONDER

People think that they have to wait until "we get over yonder," like the old song says, before we can see heaven opened and invading earth. I don't want to wait until "over yonder." I want to walk in it now. The revelatory realm of God is the unseen realm that can be seen now! I want to dwell in the intimate tent of God's glory.

THE REVELATORY REALM
IS RIGHT HERE, RIGHT NOW.

I'm going to be sharing scriptures with you that indicate the truth about portals and how this truth will enable you to walk under an open heaven in this day and time. It is up to you, to accept it as truth for your life. I usually tell people that, "If I can't back up the revelation that God has given me with His Word, then don't listen to me. But, if I can back it up with His Word, then give it a chance to change you from glory to glory" (2 Cor. 3:18). According to your faith, so be it unto you.

"Then touched he their eyes, saying, According to your faith be it unto you."

Matthew 9:29, KJV

God's prophets and prophetesses were never received well in either the Old Testament or the New Testament. Ezekiel and Jeremiah had a hard time being received by the people because of the revelation that God had given them. People aren't familiar with intimacy, so they are unfamiliar with revelation. Prophecy is when God reveals a matter to one for others to see. Revelation is revealed intimately to one in order to set him/her free and then to set others free. Revelation is God's explanation which is His Word revealed. A lot of people reject the revelation that God has shown me simply because it is not natural, it is supernatural. When applied to their lives, however, it brings massive change (change that they have prayed for) and thus fulfills their destinies. I am a destiny pusher. I push people to their destinies. A push is different from a shove. If you're not very careful, you will confuse this with being pushed. People have to have help when it comes to change, because the lack of change is the evidence of being stuck. A shove is appreciated once we realize that we have been stuck in our own misunderstanding which has allowed our destiny to be detoured.

**A GOOD SHOVE WILL HELP YOU
TO REESTABLISH YOUR DIRECTION
THROUGH REVELATORY CORRECTION.**

Change is the hardest thing to accomplish, but once it is accomplished, it is worth it. I've learned that it is okay when change is too much for people to handle, but that can't stop me from seeking more of Him and less of them. You will find out, too, as you walk in the supernatural that most people will try to rain on your parade when you share revelation, but you have to realize that their rain is the counterfeit to the reign of God's glory.

> *"The glory of this latter house shall be greater than of the former, saith the Lord of hosts: and in this place will I give peace, saith the Lord of hosts."*
>
> **Haggai 2:9, KJV**

We need to get to the place where God floods us with His glory and we stop being flooded by the emotional issues of others. I must get over myself and deal with my rejection issues so that it won't matter if someone doesn't believe the revelation that God has given me to carry. If I operate under rejection, then I can't operate under the glory.

Here are a few scriptures about rain that will help you understand the importance of allowing it to come forth in our lives. Supernatural rain comes through your portal. When I first starting carrying the glory of God, it would rain every time that I would speak about the glory. It got to the point that I would tell people, "Watch what happens when I talk about the glory of God," and it would literally rain every time.

DON'T LET OTHERS
RAIN ON YOUR PARADE.

> *I will give the rain for your land in its season, the early rain and the latter rain, that you may gather in your grain, your new wine, and your oil.*
>
> **Deuteronomy 11:14, AMP**

Yes, let us know (recognize, be acquainted with, and understand) Him; let us be zealous to know the Lord [to appreciate, give heed to, and cherish Him]. His going forth is prepared and certain as the dawn, and He will come to us as the [heavy] rain, as the latter rain that waters the earth.

Hosea 6:3, AMP

LET IT RAIN!

"Be glad then, you children of Zion, and rejoice in the Lord, your God; for He gives you the former or early rain in just measure and in righteousness, and He causes to come down for you the rain, the former rain and the latter rain, as before."

Joel 2:23, AMP

"Ask of the Lord rain in the time of the latter or spring rain. It is the Lord Who makes lightnings which usher in the rain and give men showers, and grass to everyone in the field."

Zechariah 10:1, AMP

When God explains Himself to people and they share it, it may seem different from the written Word, but it is still God's explanation. The word of God talks about the world not being able to handle all of the books if everything Jesus did had been written down.

"And there are also many other things which Jesus did, the which, if they should be written every one, I suppose that even the world itself could not contain the books that should be written. Amen."

John 21:25, KJV

Jesus told satan on the Mount of Temptation,

"But he answered and said, It is written, Man shall not live by bread alone, but by every word that proceedeth out of the mouth of God."

Matthew 4:4, KJV

Again, every word that proceedeth out of the mouth of God is revelation. Revelation is God's explanation.

John was totally abandoned and exiled before he ever received revelation. He received revelation when he understood the open portal that was over his life. This is a prime time in your life: when you think that your life is over, you must acknowledge that you are under an open portal and it will be over your life (not your life is over.) The people who exiled John thought that his life was over, when in all actuality, they shoved him into a place in his life where his portal was expanded. We will be talking more about how to expand your portal later in the book. Normal people would have died, but because John realized the revelation that was coming through His open portal, he was able to live a supernatural life in an impossible atmosphere of ostracism. He was boiled in oil, but even this didn't kill him!

Despair, when surrendered to God, brings forth an expansion of your portal. Your life isn't over but is under an open holy portal of heaven. When you understand that you are under an open heaven, then the glory and revelation of God can come through. When you receive understanding and your eyes are enlightened then your portal can be expanded. Remember,

"Wisdom is the principal thing; therefore get wisdom: and with all thy getting get understanding."

Proverbs 4:7, KJV

Revelation also comes to an individual as he or she becomes available for intimacy with God. People, who have an ear to hear the revelation of God, usually don't get supported too well by others. If others would be **open** to hear what the messenger receives, then they would benefit from the revelation that God reveals.

DESPAIR, WHEN SURRENDERED TO GOD, BRINGS FORTH AN EXPANSION OF YOUR PORTAL.

Unfortunately, when other people reject hearing what God has spoken, they often shut down and that causes them to have fear, doubt and unbelief. So many times when people won't listen to us, we shut down, but don't let that stop you from hearing God. Fear, doubt, and unbelief will block you from hearing the revelation of God, so be very careful not to let others take this from you. Just remember that God told you, and not them. The reason He told you was because they wouldn't listen to Him. The fact of the matter is that not many people hear and see revelation because of their fear, doubt, and unbelief. Fear, doubt, and unbelief have the ability to close a mind. They also have the ability to constrict a portal that would otherwise be expanded. Repentance always brings one hundred percent restoration, so may we pray?

REPENTANCE ALWAYS BRINGS RESTORATION!

Dear Heavenly Father,
I purpose and choose to repent for operating in fear, doubt, and unbelief that have disabled me from hearing Your revelation, and I also repent for how I have allowed others to influence me to the point that I feared them instead of hearing You. I desire to hear You Lord and to walk in the revelatory realm of Your glory. In Jesus' name.

CHAPTER THREE

AN OPEN MIND

History tells you what has been, prophecy tells you what will be, but revelation reveals to you the NOW. Revelation comes through an open portal; the more expanded the portal is the more revelation comes through it. We need more revelation to reveal what has been concealed throughout generations. God not only wants to give you revelation beyond His original intentions, He also wants to reveal things to us that have been hidden because they could cause us harm. Traumas are happenings that the enemy stuffs into time that steal, kill, and destroy God's people prematurely, and God ends up getting blamed.

Revelation desires to come forth through your portal, but you have to be willing to expand your mind, and then eternity can be released in this dispensation of time. I hear people all of the time say, "in God's timing." You are the entry point of eternity that can enable this to occur. Time is the enemy to eternity; therefore, traumas have to be stuffed into time. When you allow an open heaven to invade your individual era of time, then God can disable the itinerary of the enemy. There are no traumas in heaven; therefore, when we walk in the glory realm of God, we are walking in the eternal realm (no time). The evidence that traumas are stuffed into time is that when a trauma happens, things slow down as if they were happening in slow motion. This is because the enemy is stuffing traumas into time! When you walk under an open portal, you walk in the no-time zone that disables traumas from coming forth. An open mind can open time. In other words, as you open your mind to the supernatural things of God, God will open time and remove traumas that were stuffed in there by the enemy. Remember the story I shared in Chapter 1 about my grandfather. He had to open his mind so his portal could be expanded to allow his blessings to come through. The number one reason we don't walk under an open heaven is because we don't have open minds. An open mind creates a correlation of revelation that opens the heavens on your behalf.

AN OPEN MIND IS A WEAPON
TO DEFEAT THE ENEMY.

Another area of great attribution concerning an open portal is the fact that generational curses have to manifest when the heavens open over creation to bring forth revelation. Generational curses also need the revelation of God to reveal their hidden agendas of death and destruction, so God's people can be set free. A generational curse is any repetitious pattern of destruction that continues to steal, kill, and destroy. Another explanation of a generational curse is anything in your life that seems bigger than you are. If it seems larger than you are, and you have never been able to overcome it, it is because it is a curse and it has to be broken in Jesus' name. May we pray?

Dear Heavenly Father,
I purpose and choose with my free will to repent for any and
all ways that I have participated in generational curses that
have brought destruction in my life. Lord, forgive me for all the

ignorance that I have operated under that has given destruction
a right to remain. I forgive myself and ask that You would pour
forth Your revelation and glory upon me so that I may be set free.
In Jesus' name.

So many people have died premature deaths because of the lack of knowledge concerning generational curses. You can read more about generational curses in my first book, **"The Well of God's Glory Unveiled."** God has hidden mysteries in His Word that He would like to reveal to His people who have eyes to see and ears to hear. Are you interested? We have helped so many people break generational curses that would have taken their lives. Glory to God! When you have an open mind and you allow your portal to be expanded then anything is possible. We have actually seen body parts come down for people who needed them through open portals.

> *"And he said unto them, Unto you it is given to know the mystery of the kingdom of God: but unto them that are without, all these thing are done in parables: That seeing they may see, and not perceive; and hearing that they may hear, and not understand; lest at any time they should be converted, and their sins should be forgiven them."*
> **Mark 4:11-12, KJV**

This is probably an appropriate time to stop and discuss any fear, doubt, or unbelief that you may currently be experiencing. I just want to start by saying that I am not a tree hugging, kool-aid kind of preacher. Believe it or not, this was contrary to the religion that I practiced when God first introduced me to His glory. Revelation is contrary to religion, so that should challenge you to discern every matter to see if it is from the Lord or not. Time will tell, and if you go with God, then signs, wonders, and miracles will manifest around you. God's goal is to bring you out of religion and into His revelation. As I discerned every matter before the Lord, He took me into a teaching that I never would have received if I hadn't believed.

People are so afraid that they are going to get involved with new age religion or some sort of witchcraft or darkness with this teaching. Just because you have never heard it before doesn't mean that it is dark. The light of God's glory will confirm to you everything that I am teaching to you by way of His illumination. He said,

> *"Ask, and it shall be given you; seek, and ye shall find; knock, and it shall be opened unto you."*
> **Luke 11:9, KJV**

What shall be opened for you? The door, your mind, and your portal must be opened so the blessings of the Lord may flood through. We must use discernment and not judgment.

> *"Beloved, believe not every spirit, but try the spirits whether they are of God: because many false prophets are gone out into the world."*
> **1 John 4:1, KJV**

Why is it that we allow the things of the enemy to destroy us, and when it comes to a new thing that God is trying to do, we destroy it? May I lead you through a prayer?

Dear Heavenly Father,
I purpose and choose with my free will to repent for any and all ways that I have participated in fear, doubt, and unbelief that have kept me from opening my mind to what You have for me now. I ask that You forgive me for participating with things when I knew that they were untruths. I also ask that You would

forgive me for calling bad things good and good things bad in my life to keep me from having to deal with them. I forgive everyone who wrongfully led me in my life, and I release the torment of hesitation that came when You desired to introduce me to Your intimacy. Help me to open myself up to You that I may be filled and healed with Your presence. In Jesus' name.

God desires that we see, hear, and understand His revelation. Revelation is not just the last book of the Bible; it is to be heard from the heavenlies. Remember, revelation is what Jesus revealed to satan on the Mt. of Temptation.

"But He replied, It has been written, Man shall not live and be upheld and sustained by bread alone, but by every word that comes forth from the mouth of God."
Matthew 4:4, AMP

Revelation reveals hidden mysteries that have kept us from receiving all that God has for us here on earth as it is in heaven. The book of Revelation is the most misunderstood book of the Bible, simply because few people understand revelation. Again, revelation is God's explanation. We are so used to trying to figure out the Word of God, and we have had life long, unanswered questions because of our misunderstandings.

REVELATION IS AN ETERNAL EXPLANATION THAT HOLDS AN ANSWER FOR EVERYTHING.

I had several preachers that were part of my congregation, and I announced that we were going to begin a study on Revelation. One of the preachers came to me and told me, *"You can't teach on Revelation."* I said, *"Why?"* He said, *"It is too controversial, and it will cause too much trouble for the church."* I said, *"You have got to be kidding me."* I fortunately chose to deny his advice and taught Revelation anyway, and now I am walking in divine revelation daily.

> ***Blessed (happy, to be envied) is the man who reads aloud [in the assemblies] the word of this prophecy; and blessed (happy, to be envied) are those who hear [it read] and who keep themselves true to the things which are written in it [heeding them and laying them to heart], for the time [for them to be fulfilled] is near."***
>
> **Revelation 1:3, AMP**

The last report that I heard from that preacher is that he had major organ failure and a transplant that left him disabled.

REVELATION IS NOT CONTROVERSIAL, IT IS COMPLIMENTARY.

Don't you need some heaven here on earth? Open yourself up to hear from heaven, and not only hear but understand exactly what the Father is saying to you by way of revelation in this hour. Again, the Word tells us to seek and we will find, knock and the door will be opened, ask and it shall be given. This is a little exercise that works for me. Get somewhere where you are alone and quiet (alone means without any kind of electrical device: cell phone, i-Pad, etc.). Just sit still and wait for that still small voice from heaven that can change everything. God speaks by way of thoughts. Discern whether the thoughts are from Him or not.

"Beloved, Do not put faith in every spirit, but prove (test) the spirits to discover whether they proceed from God; for many false prophets have gone forth into the world."

1 John 4:1, AMP

Some scriptures I will be repeating time and time again until you get them! Acknowledge this newfound knowledge about open portals, and ask God to expand your portal so that revelation can flow through you like water flowing down a river.

"He that believeth on me, as the scripture hath said, out of his belly shall flow rivers of living water."

John 7:38, KJV

Patience is a virtue! You may have to wait a little while and relax in His presence, which is something we are not accustomed to doing. Waiting will introduce you to resting. We get aggravated if we pull through a fast food joint and have to pull around to the white line and wait for our burger. We don't serve a fast food God, so you might have to wait a little longer at His white line.

THE LONGER YOU'RE WILLING TO WAIT FOR GOD, THE LESS YOU HAVE TO.

Take a few deep breaths and release any unforgiveness, bitterness, or anger you may have. Be very careful not to assume that this does not apply to you, because the things that you think you don't have, you usually have a double portion of. We need to understand that repentance always brings restoration. Better yet, ask the King of your heart if there is anything in there that would interrupt intimacy (love)? Here are a few inner issues that you may be able to relate to:

THE VERY THING THAT YOU THINK
THAT YOU DON'T HAVE, YOU DO!

Do you have bitterness?

Do you have unforgiveness?

Do you have envy and jealousy?

Bitterness—any way that you are disgusted with yourself and others.

Unforgiveness—any way that you hold an offense against yourself and others.

Self-hatred—any way that you hate yourself, which causes you to hate others.

Fear—any unpleasant emotion that causes you to feel threatened by danger.

Rejection—any way that you refuse to be accepted.

Abandonment—any way that you exile yourself.

Self-pity—any way that you put yourself above God.

Judgment—any way that you blame others, God or yourself.

Pride—any way that you think that you are the source of soundness.

Rebellion—any way that you portray your will over God's will.

Procrastination—any way that you put off what God has put on. Delayed obedience is disobedience.

Denial—any way that you deny truth.

Regret—any way that you allow grief to relive.

Unbelief—any way that you doubt God.

Depression—any way that you have allowed anger to turn inward.

Anger—any way that you allow hostility to keep you in captivity.

Resentment—any way that you allow bitterness to take the place of intimacy.

These are just a few definitions of undealt-with, inner issues that will keep you from walking under an open portal. You must know the definition of the issue before you can have the knowledge of repentance that brings you into restoration. It wasn't until Job repented that he was restored. May I lead you through a prayer of relaxation and repentance that allows God's revelation to flow to you and through you?

Dear Heavenly Father,

I purpose and choose with my free will to relax in Your presence as I give myself a break. Lord, forgive me for being too tough on others, and myself and I forgive myself. I also ask You to forgive me for (fill in the blank with your inner issue), *and I forgive myself. Father God, I repent for any and all ways that I have kept myself from walking in Your divine revelation because of my lack of knowledge. Please forgive me for leaning on my own understanding and for not acknowledging Your revelation as the ultimate explanation. I realize that Your explanation can set me free from myself. Expand my portal that originates at Your holy throne, and rain upon me the revelation and glory that You desire for me to have, in Jesus' name. You are so good to show Your mercy and kindness to me while I work out my salvation. You alone are God, and no one else will do. I love You.*

Now take a few breaths and regroup, and see how it feels. Just know that as you walk in an open portal, the things of the unseen realm will become visible in this realm, and God will show you divine revelations and appointments that will take you to another place.

IT'S THE GLORY REALM!

I want to operate in the revelatory realm of God! The revelatory realm of God is the glorious heavenly realm invading the earthly realm. In order to witness heaven invading earth, we must operate in the glory realm of God. We must know more about God's glory as well because the bible says:

> *"For the earth shall be filled with the knowledge of the glory of the Lord, as the waters cover the sea."*
> **Habakkuk 2:14, KJV**

We must have knowledge of the glory of the Lord before we can know how to be filled as the waters cover the sea! Habakkuk says that **we** (the earth) have to be filled with the knowledge of the glory. The glory of the Lord is the unexplained, convincing, manifested presence of God. We must be filled with His presence in order to be made whole. As the glory of God rains down and invades the earth, the Word of God says that we shall all see it together.

> *"And the glory of the Lord shall be revealed, and all flesh shall see it together: for the mouth of the Lord hath spoken it."*
> **Isaiah 40:5, KJV**

Not only shall we be filled with His glory, but we shall be poured out into the earthly realm as a flood of His glory for all others to see. God desires to use us to flood the earth with His presence.

> *"Be glad then, ye children of Zion, and rejoice in the Lord your God: for he hath given you the former rain moderately, and he will cause to come down for you the rain, the former rain, and the latter rain in the first month."*
> **Joel 2:23, KJV**

THE LATTER RAIN COMES DOWN
THROUGH YOUR PORTAL.

The glory and revelation of God travel through portals from heaven to earth. If you learn how to expand your portal, the more revelation and glory you will receive. We will talk more about this later in the book. Revelation is anything that is revealed right now by God!

Another reason people don't hear more of revelation is because of fear, doubt, and unbelief. Many people assume that God only spoke to the people of the Old Testament and/or the holiest people. God wants to speak to you. He is your Father, and He wants to communicate with you on a daily basis; it's called true intimacy. If you desire to hear more revelation from God, I suggest that you take a moment and repent. Again, repentance always brings restoration! You can't go wrong by doing right! By the way, repentance is turning from the way you do things, to doing things the way God would have you to. Turn from yourself and turn towards God, and He will supply your every need.

REPENTANCE BRINGS
ONE HUNDRED PERCENT RESTORATION.

Dear Heavenly Father,
I purpose and choose with my free will to repent for any and all fear, doubt, and unbelief that I have operated under as sin in my life. Lord, I ask that you would forgive me for the ways that I have allowed these sins to control my faith level concerning You and Your kingdom here on earth, as it is in heaven. Lord, I desire to see and hear the supernatural. In order to receive Your revelation, I acknowledge that I must have an ear to hear. Lord, help me have ears to hear and eyes to see in this supernatural

hour that I live in. Lord, also help me turn from the shallow thinking that I operate in and dive into the depths of Your revelation. In Jesus' name.

Now that we have gotten all of that unbelief out of the way, may we continue? Keep in mind that throughout your walk in the supernatural, you will have to repeat this repentance prayer several times, maybe even daily. The enemy doesn't want you to have the supernatural revelation of eternal insight, so if he can distract you with fear, doubt, and unbelief, he will. Fear, doubt, and unbelief will disable you from walking in the supernatural and will also constrict your portal. Fear, doubt, and, unbelief try daily to get you to doubt what God wants you to hear or see. God is looking for a remnant of people who are willing to see and hear what the Lord says and does. I don't want to be the one who has ears to hear, but doesn't hear and eyes to see, but doesn't see. Take a look at what Jesus told His disciples:

> **"Having eyes, see ye not? and having ears, hear ye not? and do ye not remember?"**
>
> **Mark 8:18, KJV**

God is searching for a remnant of people who will hear His revelation in this critical hour. He is preparing us for what is ahead. Let us be this remnant that knows the knowledge of the glory of the Lord, that we may be used to pour it out upon our nation. Would you like to be a part of His remnant? God's revelation and glory travels through open portals. With this in mind, let's go on into the scriptures concerning the **"Portals Of Heaven."**

> **"Esaias also crieth concerning Israel, Though the number of the children of Israel be as the sand of the sea, a remnant shall be saved:"**
>
> **Romans 9:27, KJV**

PSALMS 24, AMP

1) THE EARTH is the Lord's, and the fullness of it, the world and they who dwell in it.

2) For He has founded it upon the seas and established it upon the currents and the rivers.

3) Who shall go up into the mountain of the Lord? Or who shall stand in His Holy Place?

4) He who has clean hands and a pure heart, who has not lifted himself up to falsehood or to what is false, nor sworn deceitfully.

5) He shall receive blessing from the Lord and righteousness from the God of his salvation.

6) This is the generation [description] of those who seek Him [who inquire of and for Him and of necessity require Him], who seek Your face,[O God of] Jacob. Selah [pause, and think of that]!

7) Lift up your heads, O you gates; and be lifted up, you age-abiding doors, that the King of glory may come in.

8) Who is the King of glory? The Lord strong and mighty, the Lord mighty in battle.

9) Lift up your heads, O you gates; yes, lift them up, you age-abiding doors, that the King of glory may come in.

10) Who is [He then] this King of glory? The Lord of hosts, He is the King of glory. Selah [pause, and think of that]!

There are several things that I want to point out here in the Word of God. The first thing that I feel is necessary to do is to break up these ten scriptures from Psalms 24 into two-scripture segments. Starting with scripture numbers one and two we shall begin our dissection for discussion. We must realize by way of revelation that the first scripture is declaring the **fullness** of the earth, world and those who dwell in it. It is important to go back in scripture to the origin of God's Word:

> *"THE EARTH is the Lord's, and the fullness of it, the world and they who dwell in it. For He has founded it upon the seas and established it upon the currents and the rivers."*
>
> **Psalms 24:1-2, AMP**

> *"In the beginning God created the heaven and the earth. And the earth was without form, and void; and darkness was upon the face of the deep. And the Spirit of God moved upon the face of the waters. And God said, Let there be light: and there was light. And God saw the light, that it was good: and God divided the light from the darkness."*
>
> **Genesis 1:1-4, KJV**

The words *"without form"* and *"void"* indicate emptiness. Think it not strange that we are called earthen vessels in the Word of God. Have you ever felt as if you were without form or void? Have you ever felt EMPTY? God created the earth without form and void to show us that He would and could fill us with His Presence (His Glory). In order for one to be filled, one must realize his own emptiness. Acknowledging your emptiness and His glory provides an opportunity for God's glory to fill you and make you whole. By the way, it will always be easier to observe other people's emptiness, so be very careful not to try to fix others when you are broken yourself. May we pray?

HAVE YOU EVER FELT AS IF YOU
WERE VOID AND WITHOUT FORM?

Dear Heavenly Father,
I purpose and choose with my free will to repent for any and all ways that I have tried to fix others out of my own brokenness. I realize that You alone are God, and I trust that you can fix my loved ones without my help. Help me to truly trust You with all of my heart that I may receive a heart of wisdom. In Jesus' name.

"But we have this treasure in earthen vessels, that the excellency of the power may be of God, and not of us."
2 Corinthians 4:7, KJV

We probably need to back up just a moment and clarify what the Word of God says:

"But even if our Gospel (the glad tidings) also be hidden (obscured and covered up with a veil that hinders the knowledge of God), it is hidden [only] to those who are perishing and obscured [only] to those who are spiritually dying and veiled [only] to those who are lost. For the god of this world has blinded the unbelievers' minds [that they should not discern the truth], preventing them from seeing the illuminating light of the Gospel of the glory of Christ (the Messiah), Who is the Image and Likeness of God. For what we preach is not ourselves but Jesus Christ as Lord,

and ourselves [merely] as your servants (slaves) for Jesus'
sake. For God Who said, Let light shine out of darkness,
has shone in our hearts so as [to beam forth] the Light for
the illumination of the knowledge of the majesty and glory
of God [as it is manifest in the Person and is revealed] in
the face of Jesus Christ (the Messiah). However, we possess
this precious treasure [the divine Light of the Gospel] in
[frail, human] vessels of earth, that the grandeur and ex-
ceeding greatness of the power may be shown to be from
God and not from ourselves."

2 Corinthians 4:3-7, AMP

God gave me a revelation concerning the amount of His glory
that is already within us; He desires to fill us to the point of completion. This is the veil that the bride must remove in order to see and
hear the revelation of the bridegroom. God desires to heal our land,
but first we must remove the veil that has hindered us from seeing
and hearing what God has to say to the church.

"But even unto this day, when Moses is read, the veil is
upon their heart. Nevertheless when it shall turn to the
Lord, the veil shall be taken away. Now the Lord is that
Spirit: and where the Spirit of the Lord is, there is liberty.
But we all, with open face beholding as in a glass the glory
of the Lord, are changed into the same image from glory to
glory, even as by the Spirit of the Lord."

2 Corinthians 3:15-19, KJV

In order to be changed from glory to glory, we first must come
out from underneath the veil.

WHEN WE COME OUT
FROM UNDERNEATH THE VEIL,
THEN THE GATES OF HELL
CANNOT PREVAIL.

"If My people, who are called by My name, shall humble themselves, pray, seek, crave, and require of necessity My face and turn from their wicked ways, then will I hear from heaven, forgive their sin, and heal their land."

2 Chronicles 7:14, AMP

CHAPTER FOUR

NATURAL VS. SUPERNATURAL

I give this revelation at every conference and write it in all of my material. If you can get this revelation, then you can be filled with the glory of God. Think it not strange that the earth is made up of seventy percent water. We, as earthen vessels, are also made up of seventy percent water. Water represents the Spirit of God.

> *"And it shall come to pass in the last days, saith God, I will pour out of my Spirit upon all flesh: and your sons and your daughters shall prophesy, and your young men shall see visions, and your old men shall dream dreams:"*
>
> **Acts 2:17, KJV**

Another confirmation that the Spirit is represented as water is:

> *"He that believeth on me, as the scripture hath said, out of his belly shall flow rivers of living water."*
>
> **John 7:38, KJV**

Another scripture that I like to share is what Jesus told the Samaritan woman at the well,

"Jesus answered and said unto her, Whosoever drinketh of this water shall thirst again: But whosoever drinketh of the water that I shall give him shall never thirst; but the water that I shall give him shall be in him a well of water springing up into everlasting life. The woman saith unto him, Sir, give me this water, that I thirst not, neither come hither to draw."

John 4:13-15, KJV

It is impossible to live without water in the natural and in the supernatural. The Spirit of God is represented by water in the supernatural. The Word says here in 2 Chronicles that God wants to heal our land. What is land? Anything that isn't covered by water! I asked God what land was, and He told me that it was everything that wasn't covered by His water (glory). His Spirit is His glory. The water represents His Spirit and glory.

"And one cried to another and said, Holy, holy, holy is the Lord of hosts; the whole earth is full of His glory!"

Isaiah 6:3, AMP

We see here in this passage of scripture from the angel's point of view that, "the whole earth is full of His glory." God's creation is only seventy percent full of His glory. Therefore, we must get the other thirty percent covered. We are a three part being according to the Word of God.

"And the very God of peace sanctify you wholly; and I pray God your whole spirit and soul and body be preserved blameless unto the coming of our Lord Jesus Christ."

1 Thessalonians 5:23, KJV

SPIRIT, BODY AND SOUL

Again, this is revelation that God gave me concerning us getting our land healed. Remember, revelation is God's explanation. The Spirit of God is represented by water, and we are seventy percent water. Then that means that we are filled with seventy percent spirit. The part that is considered land is the remaining thirty percent, which is made up of two segments: fifteen percent body and fifteen percent soul. The body makes up our physical being. Our soul is made up of mind, will, emotions, memory and imagination. If we have a physical affliction, we need to pray for our soul to be healed.

REVELATION WILL ALWAYS BE CONTRARY TO RELIGION!

I know that this sounds contrary, but our body will obey our mind. The land in this passage of scripture is our body and soul. When we get our land covered by the Spirit (glory), then we will be filled. We need a filling not a feeling!

"For the earth shall be filled with the knowledge of the glory of the Lord, as the waters cover the sea."
Habakkuk 2:14, KJV

It is now time that our earthen vessel be filled, healed and made one hundred percent whole. The only places that one can be sick are the soul and body. There can be no sickness in the Spirit realm! Hallelujah.

70% WATER (SPIRIT)
15% BODY (PHYSICAL)
15% SOUL (MIND, WILL, EMOTIONS)
_____

100% WHOLENESS

"The earth is the Lord's, and the fulness thereof; the world, and they that dwell therein."

Ps. 24:1, KJV

In the beginning the earth was without form and void, but now we see in Psalms 24:1 that the **earth is full**. Full of what? The fullness thereof. It says that the fullness of it (being the earth) can be dwelled in. Only when we dwell in Him, can we walk in fullness. In other words, the earth is the Lord's and the fullness thereof means that even though the earth was created void and without form, the fullness thereof was still available. The reason that many times we don't receive our healing is because we just assume that God will fill us, when in all actuality, we need to realize that His fullness is what our emptiness needs. There was a process that the earth went through in order to become full. This process occurred when the emptiness of the earth was realized by its own existence, and then God could begin to fill it with His splendor and majesty, which is His glory.

If we would let God fulfill us, then the seventy percent of His spirit that already exists within us would become one hundred percent, and we would be made whole. In other words, we can be flooded with God's wholeness, which is His love. When God looks down on us, He sees the seventy percent of Himself that is made up by His Spirit. God cannot look upon sin.

"Behold, The Lord's hand is not shortened at all, that it cannot save, nor His ear dull with deafness, that it cannot hear. But your iniquities have made a separation between you and your God, and your sins have hidden His face from you, so that He will not hear."

Is. 59:1-2, AMP

When God looks upon us, He sees the seventy percent of Himself because it is in the form of water (His Spirit), and water reflects

Him. If we would allow Him to fill us, then He could see one hundred percent of Himself instead of seventy percent. In other words, if we would get over ourselves (30% land, soul-body) and allow God to flood us with His glory, then when He looked upon us He would see one hundred percent of Himself. Don't you know that God is ready to see one hundred percent of Himself in His children?

I had a science project one time that proved this to be true, I dug a small hole in the ground, and within a few months the hole had filled itself in. This tells me that God is more than able to fill in any emptiness that abounds. Emptiness attracts emptiness, unless there is a greater force field of wholeness.

EMPTINESS IS THE EVIDENCE OF A NEED TO BE FILLED.

The power of God is already in us working the supernatural. We just have to realize that our emptiness requires a filling (not a feeling) if we are to continue to the place of wholeness that brings holiness.

"Now unto him that is able to do exceeding abundantly above all that we ask or think, according to the power that worketh in us."

Ephesians 3:20, KJV

FEELINGS BREAK US. FILLINGS MAKE US.

This is the process that God shared with me concerning emptiness:

1. We must first realize our own emptiness.
2. We must analyze our emptiness without blaming others, ourselves, or God.
3. We must repent of our emptiness and make ourselves available to be healed and filled by God's glory.

Once you realize that you are broken and empty and stop defending it, you can then move on to the next phase. This phase consists of you not blaming yourself, God, or others. Sin is at fault. Then after you get to this place, you can go deeper and know that once you repent, restoration will restore your very soul.

"Deep calleth unto deep at the noise of thy waterspouts: all thy waves and thy billows are gone over me."

Ps. 42:7, KJV

May I lead you in a prayer?

Dear Heavenly Father,
I purpose and choose with my free will to repent for any and all ways that I have blamed others for my emptiness. I realize that my emptiness is an expression of my own insecurities and anxieties that I have protected instead of making them available for deliverance. Please help me to see all the areas in my life where my emptiness has created holes, and I ask that You would fill all of my emptiness with Your fullness and wholeness. In Jesus' Name.

We must first realize that our present day condition was introduced to us as sin at the fall of mankind. Between the iniquities of our forefathers and sharing the womb with sin, we have had a hard time achieving wholeness.

"Keeping mercy for thousands, forgiving iniquity and transgression and sin, and that will by no means clear the guilty; visiting the iniquity of the fathers upon the children, and upon the children's children, unto the third and to the fourth generation."

Ex. 34:7, KJV

"Behold, I was brought forth in [a state of] iniquity; my mother was sinful who conceived me [and I too am sinful]."

Ps. 51:5, AMP

Since our conception, the enemy has been trying hard to keep us empty because he knows that if we are filled and healed, then his kingdom in our life will fall.

These scriptures tell me that I was conceived in sin. Sin brings separation, and separation causes death. Separation is the defining line of complications that hinder completion. God did not create the earth without form and void to prove brokenness to humanity, but to prove wholeness to us. We, as humans, must realize our frailties without the judgment of fault. Separation is cracks that have interrupted the foundation of our faith in God. Cracks are crooked lines within one's foundation that allow chaos to have a direction to follow. The crooked and cracked places of your life are the areas where emptiness can dwell. It's time that we identify the emptiness and evict it and welcome wholeness to move in. The Word of God states that Jesus came to make the crooked places straight (Is. 45:2). You can't operate in complication and expect completion.

Completion comes from within the deep places of our beings that only God can heal. When a wound heals, it heals from the inside out. If we are separated from God, then His glory (light) cannot reach the deep places within us that need His Presence to bring completion. The glory can only go into the dark places where we allow God in. The evidences of these places are: feelings of loneliness that accompany the thoughts of never being healed in the desperate depths of oneself and the enemy saying that there is no hope for your healing. You may have even given up on a healing in these places and learned to live with infirmities in order to survive. My friend, He desires for wholeness to invade your emptiness. An expansion of your portal is exactly what you need to deliver you in this most desperate hour. May we pray?

Dear Heavenly Father,
I purpose and choose with my free will to repent for any and all
ways that I have neglected expansion to offer myself to emptiness.
I thank You Lord that I now have knowledge of how to expand
my portal that Your glory can come through in my life in an
amazing way. Teach me how to walk under an open heaven of
Your glory that others and I may be set free. In Jesus' name.

HAVE YOU EVER OWNED A MOUNTAIN?

We have become our own mountain. We have become like the
Israelites circling the same mountain, wondering around in this wil-
derness of life. The word of God says,

> **"And Jesus said unto them, Because of your unbelief: for**
> **verily I say unto you, If ye have faith as a grain of mus-**
> **tard seed, ye shall say unto this mountain, Remove hence**
> **to yonder place; and it shall remove; and nothing shall be**
> **impossible unto you."**
>
> **Matt.17:20, KJV**

A mustard seed is the smallest of all seeds unless it gets stuck between your teeth, and then it feels like the largest seed in the world.
This is the revelation that God gave me concerning us becoming
our own mountain. The Israelites kept circling the mountain because of their unbelief and doubt. In other words, they continued
to walk in circles because they couldn't believe for themselves. They
thought that they had to have a leader, so if things went wrong
they would not have to take responsibility. The Lord told me that,
"they couldn't get over themselves." The journey was only supposed to take a few days, and it ended up taking forty years. If
they had "mustered up" enough courage to go over the mountain,
the promised land was just on the other side. They were their own

mountain. Why do we continuously circle our inner issues in life instead of conquering them and getting over ourselves? It should have only taken a few days but instead it has taken years…

WE MUST GET OVER OURSELF!

You may not know how to get over yourself, so you have to ask God to give you revelation that takes you over your own mountain. We all have mountains in life; no one is exempt. When you get on top of your mountain, you can see your promises on the other side. The Israelites didn't want to go up to the mountaintop because it was too convenient in the valley. They were content with Moses ascending the mountain and then descending to bring them God's message. Unfortunately, you can't always depend on others to get your a message from God because eventually you will doubt, if you don't get a word for yourself. If a mountain is before you and you go over it, geographically where does the mountain end up? Behind you! Congratulations my friend, you just moved a mountain! God calls us to be a fountain of living waters, not a mountain. Mountains can't hold water, only fountains can! Now is the time for us, the remnant, to dive into our inner healing and allow God to fill us from within so that we may become that fountain of life springing forth from the depths of who God created us to be. This may not make any sense to some of you, but for the ones who thought that they could never be healed, this is good news. This is for you! This is for the desperate Dans and Divas in life. God is about to bring your mountain down low and make the crooked places straight.

> *"Every valley shall be lifted and filled up, and every mountain and hill shall be made low; and the crooked and uneven shall be made straight and level, and the rough places a plain."*
>
> **Isaiah 40:4, AMP**

The next scripture tells us plainly that, after this occurs, we shall then see the glory of the Lord and all flesh shall see it together. The evidence of one being filled is that it can be seen by others. In other words, you will not have to convince others that you have something that you don't!!!

"And the glory (majesty and splendor) of the Lord shall be revealed, and all flesh shall see it together; for the mouth of the Lord has spoken it."

Isaiah 40:5, AMP

If we have areas within us that are separated from completion, we need to open ourselves up to the glory of God (the light of God) to seal up and heal up our brokenness. If you have decided that this is the way it is, and if God wants it to be different, then He will have to change it, God can't change it without changing you. The Israelites kept walking around their mountain instead of walking over it. Let's realize that we are our own mountain and let us conquer the very things that hinder us from getting over ourselves. The ways we have walked around the brokenness that is within us, is only a fraction of the justification that we have operated in and called it waiting on God. Wake up and realize that the reason you settled it and walked around it is the fact that it is not your stuff. It is the stuff that you were conceived in and the stuff that came in through the loins of your forefathers. The Word of God tells me that the sins of our forefathers would visit up to the third and fourth generation. (Ex. 34:7)

The revelation of God (once you learn how to listen to Him) will take you as deep as you are willing to go. God doesn't hide mysteries in His Word to keep you from finding them: He hides things that would cause you to seek Him. God likes to play hide and go seek with His children just like you enjoy playing hide and go seek with your kids. Some people may say, "Well, I don't like to play hide and go seek," but the Word of God says that those who seek shall find. Maybe you should try it!

> **"Keep on asking and it will be given you; keep on seeking and you will find; keep on knocking [reverently] and [the door] will be opened to you."**
>
> **Matthew 7:7, AMP**

What kind of door will be opened? Keep this in mind as we continue seeking the revelation of God's Word. We have to be made whole from generational curses that have come to us by way of our ancestors. Mom and Dad did a good job raising us, but the few mistakes that were made have kept us in a broken state that has prevented us from carrying the glory of God. We can't continue to blame our parents for our present day mistakes. If we continue to blame other people, we will never take accountability for ourselves. You must realize that you are your own problem before you will learn that it's up to you to repent. Let's forgive our parents and/ or other authority figures, identify our emptiness, evict it, and be healed with God's wholeness.

Dear Father God,
I purpose and choose with my free will to repent for any and all ways that I have held unforgiveness in my heart towards my parents, grandparents or any other authority figure in my life. I forgive them for all the hurt and pain that they caused me throughout my life, and I want to release them now from my unforgiveness. Thank You God for forgiving me, so I can forgive them and myself.

I don't know about you, my friend, but more than anything else in my life I want to learn how to get over myself and carry the glory of God. Presently, we don't know a lot about the glory of God because very few people are carrying the glory of God. The Word of God says that there is a time coming when the earth will be filled with the knowledge of the glory of the Lord. In order to see and carry the glory, we (the creation of God) must learn how to operate in and acknowledge the revelatory realm of God. I recite this scripture often concerning being filled with the knowledge of the glory as the waters cover the sea.

"For the earth shall filled with the knowledge of the glory of the Lord, as the waters cover the sea."
Habakkuk 2:14, KJV

So, if there was not enough confirmation of configuration already, here is more evidence that we were born like the earth was created, void and without form. Most people walk through their whole lives not finding their purpose and end up dying prematurely because they were not made whole. God's idea is to make you (His creation) whole (here on earth) by way of you realizing the need for Him to heal you (supernaturally). Religion makes it complicated, but revelation makes it interesting. Genesis 1:1 states the emptiness of the earth but Psalms 24:1 states the fullness thereof. Let's continue. The Word of God says that when our bodies die, they return as dust to the earth, but our spirit goes back from which it came.

"Then shall the dust return to the earth as it was: and the spirit shall return unto God who gave it."
Ecclesiastes 12:7, KJV

Our bodies go as dust to the earth, and our spirits go back where they came from through our portal. What do you mean, "Where they came from?" Your spirit has already been with God in heaven, and that's why you know that you know God. I had an atheist friend tell me one time that he didn't believe in God, but when he was around me, he testified that, "somehow he knew that God was real." Atheists know God because their spirit has already been with God before the foundations of this world. Besides, it is common knowledge that you first have to believe that there is a God before you can say that you don't believe in Him. My dad always told me when I was a child that it doesn't take a lot of common sense to figure out the truth!

May we continue on with the second scripture in Psalms 24:2?

"For He has founded it upon the seas and established it upon the currents and the rivers."

Ps. 24:2, AMP

God poured Himself out in the beginning of Genesis. The Word clearly states that He hovered over the face of the deep.

"And the earth was without form, and void; and darkness was upon the face of the deep. And the Spirit of God moved upon the face of the waters."

Genesis 1:2, KJV

First, we have to consider the **FACE OF THE DEEP**. The face of the deep refers to the deepest, darkest cracks and crevasses of the earth that were broken and without form (purpose). There was no darkness, (like we know it) before God created an earth that was without form. Darkness, before the fall, wasn't evil because it was not yet separated from the light. Darkness became evil only because of the fall. God created this formless earth with fallen man in mind. In order for darkness to be present, there must be a form of bro-kenness. Shadows are formed when there is less light; total darkness forms because of the total absence of light. When light overshadows an object, the shadow forms darkness. Portals are passages that allow the light of God's glory to come to earth to overshadow darkness.

Portals are shafts of light that make their way through darkness to overshadow God's creation. As you acknowledge the glory of God in your life, you will begin seeing more portals around you manifest in your presence. God desires for us, His children, to see Him in all of His glory.

PORTALS TRANSPORT THE BLESSINGS OF GOD TO EARTH FROM THE HEAVENLIES.

We have a mindset that God does not create broken things, but God can create whatever He chooses to create because He is God. If you don't think that He can create broken things just look into the mirror. He didn't create the brokenness, but He did create you so that you could overcome brokenness. He created this formless earth with cracks and crevasses so that He could show the world that He is able to fill the dark, empty, void, and formless places of our earthen vessels.

The light, however, was not formed until there was a need for darkness to be overshadowed. This revelation creates a new look at the reality of God, He will meet you exactly where you are. Portals are God's way of transporting light from eternity to the earth, which operates in time. There is no time or distance in the glory of God through His portals simply because it is eternity extending down into time. This is God's way of allowing heaven to invade earth. For God has founded His fullness upon the seas and established it upon the currents and the rivers in order to flood us with His glory in the driest hour that mankind has ever known.

"For He has founded it upon the seas and established it upon the currents and the rivers."

Ps. 24:2, AMP

In order to understand this revelation, you have to roll up your religious pants because you are about to get soaked. I feel sure that if it has been established upon the waters, then that puts us in flood status. These are the days as Noah!

"And [just] as it was in the days of Noah, so will it be in the time of the Son of Man."

Luke 17:26, AMP

A flood of God's glory is about to sweep across our nation and saturate us with the unexplained, convincing manifestation of His presence. His GLORY! Let it rain, God, let it rain.

"Be glad then, you children of Zion, and rejoice in the Lord, your God; for He gives you the former or early rain in just measure and in righteousness, and He causes to come down for you the rain, the former rain and the latter rain, as before."

Joel 2:23, AMP

You can't get wet with God's revelation while standing under an umbrella of religion.

IT'S TIME TO PUT OUR UMBRELLAS
OF RELIGION UP
AND
LET
IT
RAIN.

CHAPTER FIVE

AN OPEN HEAVEN

There are many scriptural references in this chapter that I will be sharing with you concerning **"Portals Of Heaven."** A portal is an open heaven! How do we experience an open portal? This subject is not often spoken of simply because not many people have knowledge about this subject. I am intrigued with the truth that the heavens above can be opened for our benefit. The next two scriptures that we will be discussing are Psalms 24:3-4,

> *"Who shall go upon the mountain of the Lord? Or who shall stand in His Holy Place?"*
>
> **Ps. 24:3, KJV**

These are two questions that David, the psalmist, asked about God's creation. When questions are answered by way of revelation, then they become options. David had experienced the heavenlies opening, apparently because he was direct about his questions, and it had become an option for him to operate under an open heaven. Who shall ascend upon the hill of the Lord? David is asking the question here of **who** shall ascend upon the hill of the Lord? He had experienced **ascending** up into a holy place himself making it possible for him to ask such a question. This is what I refer to as going up into the glory. I have ascended several times and have actually seen heavenly things that I would explain as I was seeing them only for them to come to pass a few days later. I don't usually share these supernatural ascensions with many people because they may think that I have lost my marbles. For those that want more of the supernatural, it is very encouraging to hear of someone else's experience. I will give you an example of times that you may have ascended:

Have you ever been driving and realized all of the sudden that you were five or ten miles down the road and you didn't remember driving. It's like a fog or haze (some people call it daydreaming), but it is actually a supernatural ascension. If it were not supernatural, you would have hit a tree or an oncoming automobile while in the absence of your natural abilities. The fact is, God allowed you to ascend into His glory while keeping everything in alignment in the earthly realm. You may be thinking to yourself, "Well, I don't know about this." According to your faith so be it unto you, but John the revelator went up into the glory while maintaining his natural position on the isle of Patmos. Why would God do it for John and not do it for you?

> *"After this I looked, and, behold, a door was opened in heaven: and the first voice which I heard was as it were of a trumpet talking with me; which said, Come up hither, and I will shew thee things which must be hereafter."*
>
> **Rev. 4:1, KJV**

When God allows you to go into an open heaven, it is to show you things that will benefit you and others, all for the glory of God.

There is a certain place between where we live and the neighboring county where my son goes to school. Every morning when we top the hill and go around a particular curve, we look back over our left shoulders to see the glory of God. We know every day that as we pass this particular place we will see the glory, and I have told my Bible study students that this place is under an open heaven (a portal). A couple of weeks ago, we passed this place only to see hundreds of thousands of white butterflies. It was a phenomenon! There were so many white butterflies that it looked like snow on the ground, but they move up and down with a rhythm. The local newspaper did an article on this rare and bizarre happening, and now people are traveling to this place to see this beautiful sight. When you are under an open portal, butterflies gather as a sign of your new creation because you are soaring in your beauty.

BEAUTY ATTRACTS BEAUTY!

On the contrary, psychics ascend into a demonic portal to gather information to obtain personal gain. Why aren't Christians accessing their eternal rights here on this earth realm? When Christians dwell in the valley and desire that someone else bring them a word, they will read the weekly horoscope in the local paper. If you have had experiences with the demonic realm which includes psychics, horoscopes, Ouija boards, tarot cards, etc., or better yet, if you have operated in rebellion (which we all have) you have participated in witchcraft.

> *"For rebellion is as the sin of witchcraft, and stubbornness is as iniquity and idolatry. Because thou hast rejected the word of the Lord, he hath also rejected thee from being king."*
> **1 Sam. 15:23, KJV**

I would suggest that you allow me to lead you through a prayer of repentance.

Dear Heavenly Father,
I purpose and choose with my free will to repent for any and all ways that I have participated in witchcraft, pride and stubborn-ness instead of operating in Your love. Forgive me for searching

for other avenues of information concerning my individuality
instead of paying the price and walking in Your truth. I cancel
all debts that have accrued by way of my ignorance and ask that
You set me free from me. In Jesus' name.

SHADRACH, MESHACH AND ABEDNEGO

I tell the story of going up into the glory and seeing Shadrach, Meshach and Abednego and how the flames on the outside looked like they were going to destroy me. I felt as if it were okay to walk into the flames, and once on the inside, it looked like a curtain of liquid gold. Again, from the outside it looked as if it was going to destroy me, but from the inside the fire was a wall of protection. The whole time that I was ascending, I was carrying on a conversation with the three people around me (in the natural) and telling them everything that I saw. In the glory, there is no time or distance so I couldn't explain to them if I was there with Shadrach, Meshach and Abednego or if they were here with me. Either way it was an awesome experience!

Some people say to me, "Well, you're not supposed to be contacting the dead." I'm not. God allows me to see these things through my open portal. The things that I see are alive. This is the supernatural of God as I didn't ask to see Shadrach and the boys, but God apparently wanted me to see them to learn of His glory. People often doubt the glory stories that I share and I challenge them by asking them how they believe in a God that they have never seen before? It is by experience. When you experience God, do you go to Him or does He come to you? In the supernatural realm of God's glory, things just are. Remember, the glory is the <u>unexplained</u>, <u>convincing</u> manifestation of God's presence. The evidence of the supernatural is that man cannot explain it yet it is convincing! God is God and He can show you anything that He desires. So many times we lack experience because of the lack of faith.

"Ye ask, and receive not, because ye ask amiss, that ye may consume it upon your lusts."

James 4:3, KJV

How would I even have the courage to stand before thousands of people and testify if it was an untruth? If I was trying to lie about these glory stories, what would it profit me? The fact is that God allowed me to experience these things and that makes it truth enough for me.

"He that hath clean hands, and a pure heart; who hath not lifted his soul unto vanity, nor sworn deceitfully."

Ps. 24:4, KJV

The rest of this verse has to do with when you go into this place you desire to be cleaner and purer than you have ever been. It is a holy place where every tear brings cleansing. The scripture goes on to say that, "who hath not lifted up his soul unto vanity, nor sworn deceitfully." In other words, God would not let me go into these places of His glory if I were going to try to use these experiences for my own vanity. In this glorious place of an open heaven, you get straight with the useless hours of vanity that we have invested in ourselves that have still left us ugly and empty. While we are on the subject of vanity, we might as well talk about it some. Vanity is the entrance into insanity. God shares His glory with no man!

"I am the Lord: that is my name: and my glory will I not give to another, neither my praise to graven images."

Isaiah 42:8, KJV

God desires to give His glory to the ones who humble themselves, pray, seek His face, and turn from their ways so He can hear from heaven, forgive them of their sins and heal their land. He also desires for us to experience His supernatural portals that we may share them with others that they, too, can have more of Him. There is a process for carrying the glory of God; I went through this process and it was one of the greatest experiences in my life. You can read more glory stories and hear about my life-changing experience in my first book, **"The Well Of God's Glory Unveiled"**. Another illustration of an open heaven is when Stephen was being stoned.

> *"And they stoned Stephen, calling upon God, and saying, Lord Jesus, receive my spirit. And he kneeled down, and cried with a loud voice, Lord, lay not this sin to their charge. And when he had said this, he fell asleep."*
>
> **Acts 7:59-60, KJV**

The heavens opened over Stephen in the midst of the enemy stoning him, and he fell asleep. Talking about resting in the midst of persecution! This is an example of the rest of God that comes when we are under an open heaven. The word of God also clearly speaks of the two witnesses in Revelation who will ascend into their portals.

> *"And they heard a great voice from heaven saying unto them, Come up hither. And they ascended up to heaven in a cloud; and their enemies beheld them."*
>
> **Rev. 11:12, KJV**

Jacob experienced his portal as it expanded and the angels of the Lord were ascending and descending.

> *"And he dreamed that there was a ladder set up on the earth, and the top of it reached to heaven; and the angels of God were ascending and descending on it!"*
>
> **Gen. 28:12, AMP**

It frightened him because he had never experienced anything quite like it before. When God reveals the supernatural to us it may startle us at first simply because we have never experienced the supernatural, but don't be afraid to look into the realm of eternity. You may see your angels ascending and descending!

> *"He was afraid and said, How to be feared and reverenced is this place! This is none other than the house of God, and this is the gateway to heaven!"*
>
> **Gen. 28:17, AMP**

This is confirmation that it was an open heaven when Jacob said, **"This is the gateway to heaven."** Glory to God!

> *"He shall receive the blessing from the Lord, and righteousness from the God of his salvation. This is the generation of them that seek him, that seek thy face, O Jacob. Selah."*
>
> **Ps. 24:5-6, KJV**

This is the generation that will receive the revelation as Jacob did about the open portal. As a matter of fact, this is the first confirmation in the Word of God of man experiencing an open portal. That is why Psalms 24:6 states that, *"this is the generation of those who seek thy face, O Jacob"*. This is also why David wrote about it in the manner that he did, because he recognized the open portal in Jacob's life as well as his own.

> *"Lift up your heads, O ye gates; and be ye lift up, ye everlasting doors; and the King of glory shall come in. Who is this King of glory?" The Lord strong and mighty, the Lord mighty in battle."*
>
> **Ps. 24:7-8, KJV**

Why is David telling us to lift up our heads in this passage of scripture? Our heads are the highest part of our earthen vessel. Our head is the gateway to our soul. You have more openings on your head than anywhere else in your entire body. You have your ear gate, eye gate, mouth gate, and nose gate. Lift up your opening and the King of glory shall come in. *"Who is the King of Glory?"* We have to know Him as the King of glory; however, few people know Him as the King of glory. *"The Lord strong and mighty, the Lord mighty in battle."* When we open our gates, the King of glory comes in, and He fights our battles for us.

THERE IS NO WARFARE
IN THE GLORY OF GOD.

This next scripture indicates the very first opening over mankind.

"In the six hundredth year of Noah's life, in the second month, the seventeenth day of the month, the same day were all the fountains of the great deep broken up, and the windows of heaven were opened."

Gen. 7:11, KJV

"Lift up your heads, O ye gates; even lift them up, ye ever-lasting doors; and the King of glory shall come in. Who is this King of glory? The Lord of hosts, he is the King of glory. Selah."

Ps. 24:9-10, KJV

Again David is advising us to lift up our heads that the King of glory may come in. We are also reminded in Psalms 84:10 that we are the doorkeeper to our portal.

"For a day in thy courts is better than a thousand. I had rather be a doorkeeper in the house of my God, than to dwell in the tents of wickedness."

Ps. 84:10, KJV

So many times we open the door to things that are not of the Lord, it is high time that we open wide the gates of glory where the King can enter in.

"And the key of the house of David will I lay upon his shoulder; so he shall open and none shall shut; and he shall shut and none shall open."

Is. 22:22, KJV

It's time for God's people to walk through the open door that God has opened for our eyes to see and our ears to hear and to shut any doors that have been fictitiously opened.

Dear Heavenly Father,
I purpose and choose with my free will to repent for any and all doors that I have walked through that You did not ordain and choose for my life. Help me to see and hear the open heaven that You have placed over me as a portal to Your throne of grace. Help me to overcome any and all fear, doubt, and unbelief that has kept me from experiencing the supernatural. In Jesus' name.

Jesus walked under an open heaven with others experiencing it at His baptism.

"Now when all the people were baptized, and when Jesus also had been baptized, and [while He was still] praying, the [visible] heaven was opened And the Holy Spirit descended upon Him in bodily form like a dove, and a voice

*came from heaven, saying, You are My Son, My Beloved!
In You I am well pleased and find delight!"*

Luke 3:21-22, AMP

One of the things I enjoy about walking under an open portal is the fact that God shows me the ways that I have delighted Him, and in that I rejoice. There is nothing to compare to hearing your Father's approval.

I love the story that is recorded in Luke 24 of Jesus appearing to the disciples as they walked down the road to Emmaus but they did not recognize Him. God gave me revelation that the disciples recognized Jesus in the anointing but did not recognize Him in the glory. There is a difference in the anointing and the glory. Jesus said,

*"Verily, verily, I say unto you, He that believeth on me, the
works that I do shall he do also; and greater works than
these shall he do; because I go unto my Father."*

John 14:12, KJV

He is talking about the glory! The anointing took Jesus to the cross, but the glory took Him from the cross. The glory will take you into places that are greater than the things that you have already experienced with God. The glory will open your eyes to the supernatural realm that you have never before seen. Suddenly, after the disciples' eyes were opened, He vanished from their sight.

*"When their eyes were [instantly] opened and they [clearly]
recognized Him, and He vanished (departed invisibly)."*

Luke 24:31, AMP

HE WENT UP IN HIS PORTAL.
HOW MUCH CLEARER CAN IT GET!!!

I am amazed at the scriptures that are packed with the revelation of open portals. I never knew until God gave me this revelation that open portals even existed. I love this one that is found in Matthew 17.

"And after six days Jesus taketh Peter, James, and John his brother, and bringeth them up into an high mountain apart, And was transfigured before them: and his face did shine as the sun, and his raiment was white as the light. And, behold, there appeared unto them Moses and Elias talking with him. Then answered Peter, and said unto Jesus, Lord, it is good for us to be here: if thou wilt, let us make here three tabernacles; one for thee, and one for Moses, and one for Elias. While he yet spake, behold, a bright <u>cloud</u> overshadowed them: and behold a voice out of the <u>cloud</u>, which said, This is my beloved Son, in whom I am well pleased; hear ye him. And when the disciples heard it, they fell on their face, and were sore afraid. And Jesus came and touched them, and said, Arise, and be not afraid. And when they had lifted up their eyes, they saw no man, save Jesus only. And as they came down from the mountain, Jesus charged them, saying, Tell the vision to no man, until the Son of man be risen again from the dead."

Matt. 17:1-9, KJV

There is a lot of portal action going on here. Jesus' portal brought forth another validation of His father's approval. Elijah and Moses appeared in their portals, and it scared the living daylights out of the disciples. The disciples were not familiar with open portals and were frightened by the illumination that changed the very appearance of Jesus. When your portal expands, it will change your countenance as you are transformed from glory to glory.

PORTALS BRING FORTH THE FATHER'S APPROVAL.

The Word of God says:

"Keep on asking and it will be given you; keep on seeking and you will find; keep on knocking [reverently] and [the door] will be opened to you."

Matt. 7:7, AMP

What door? The door to your portal! Let's keep reading,

"Enter through the narrow gate; for wide is the gate and spacious and broad is the way that leads away to destruction, and many are those who are entering through it. But the gate is narrow (contracted by pressure) and the way is straitened and compressed that leads away to life, and few are those who find it."

Matt. 7:13-14, AMP

You have the power to either expand your portal or constrict it. The more that you expand your portal, the more glory can come through.

Have you ever seen anyone who glowed with the radiance of God's beauty? When one acknowledges the glory of God and expands his/her portal, then the shekinah glory will illuminate their very being. It is contagious; I call it Peter's shadow.

"So that they [even] kept carrying out the sick into the streets and placing them on couches and sleeping pads, [in the hope] that as Peter passed by, at least his shadow might fall on some of them."

Acts 5:15, AMP

Peter was walking under an open portal to the extent that when he walked by people his shadow healed their sicknesses. This was his portal overshadowing others, and that affected their afflictions. What a powerful personality!

We see an awesome illustration of Daniel's portal in Daniel 6.

> *"Then the king commanded, and Daniel was brought and cast into the den of lions. The king said to Daniel, May your God, Whom you are serving continually, deliver you! And a stone was brought and laid upon the mouth of the den, and the king sealed it with his own signet and with the signet of his lords, that there might be no change of purpose concerning Daniel. Then the king went to his palace and passed the night fasting, neither were instruments of music or dancing girls brought before him; and his sleep fled from him. Then the king arose very early in the morning and went in haste to the den of lions. And when he came to the den and to Daniel, he cried out in a voice of anguish. The king said to Daniel, O Daniel, servant of the living God, is your God, Whom you serve continually, able to deliver you from the lions? Then Daniel said to the king, O king, live forever!"*
>
> **Dan. 6:16-21, AMP**

Daniel had previously expanded his portal by having an excellent spirit. An excellent spirit will expand a portal every time. Evidence of excellence is always looking for a better way for yourself and others.

> *"Then this Daniel was distinguished above the presidents and the satraps because an excellent spirit was in him, and the king thought to set him over the whole realm."*
>
> **Dan. 6:3, AMP**

EXCELLENCE IS ALWAYS
DOING YOUR BEST.

The amount of glory that was able to flow through the holy portal over Daniel's life caused the lions to be at peace with him. If it caused an animal to be at peace, what would it have done for a human? When we carry an open portal over our lives, people who normally have things against us will find no case. Glory to God!

I want to share with you another character in the Bible who carried an open portal. Moses. Moses was placed in the Nile River as a three-month-old child and he fell into the hands of Pharaoh who had decreed death over him. Raised in the Egyptian palace as royalty, Moses knew there was more to his destiny. Moses murdered a man, fled from Pharaoh, and ended up marrying the daughter of a wealthy herdsman. He worked for his father-in-law and saw the glory of God in the burning bush on the backside of Mt. Horeb. God called him from out of the bush and told him to go back to Pharaoh and demand that he let His people go. He had many issues yet he carried an open portal to the extent that the glory consumed his very being. People then rejected what he carried, his portal was constricted, and his destiny was canceled.

MOSES KNEW THAT THERE
WAS MORE TO HIS DESTINY.

Be very careful not to let other people cause you to constrict your portal and cancel your destiny. The fear of what others may say about you and/or the fear of others rejecting you because of what you believe. Fear, doubt and unbelief can constrict your portal. The way to expand your portal is through faith, love, hope, unforgiveness, and kindness. All of the fruits of the Spirit found in Galatians 5 will expand your portal.

"But the fruit of the Spirit is love, joy, peace, longsuffering, gentleness, goodness, faith, Meekness, temperance: against such there is no law."

Gal. 5:22-23, KJV

A listing of things that can constrict your portal can also in found in Galatians.

"Now the works of the flesh are manifest, which are these; Adultery, fornication, uncleanness, lasciviousness, Idolatry, witchcraft, hatred, variance, emulations, wrath, strife, seditions, heresies."

Gal. 5:19-20, KJV

Moses didn't get to enter into his destiny here on earth because he allowed the people's influence to interrupt him. The cool thing about Moses is that he operated under an open heaven to the extent that when his body was laid to rest it did not decay.

"Yet Michael the archangel, when contending with the devil he disputed about the body of Moses, durst not bring against him a railing accusation, but said, The Lord rebuke thee."

Jude 1:9, KJV

I believe that if Moses had discerned the distractions of the people, he would have exited as Elijah did. I believe that you can live under an open portal to the point that you can just ascend into eternity. You may be thinking to yourself that this is too much for me. It is too much for me as well, but I like the supernatural a lot more than I do the natural, so I'm going to go with it! The natural is boring when compared to the supernatural. It should be normal for Christians to walk in the supernatural. We are just sojourners here in the natural, but you must have knowledge of the supernatural in order to walk in it. If you walk in something that you have no knowledge of, then you walk in ignorance. I am tired of being destroyed for my lack of knowledge. How about Enoch?

"And Enoch walked [in habitual fellowship] with God; and he was not, for God took him [home with Him]."

Gen. 5:24, AMP

Enoch was and then was not. He went up through his holy portal to heaven.

It is obvious that Elijah walked under an open portal.

"And it came to pass, as they still went on, and talked, that, behold, there appeared a chariot of fire, and horses of fire, and parted them both asunder; and Elijah went up by a whirlwind into heaven."

2 Kings 2:11, KJV

He went up into his open portal: what do you think about that? He did not taste death! Sounds like a good trip to me. If you are going to believe some of the Bible, you are going to have to believe all of the Bible. I know that I have thrown some heavy revelation at you in this book, but if we would just realize that the Word of God is full of heavy revelation, we could be set free by it. I have added an excerpt from my book, "**Quotes Birthed Out Of The Revelation Of God's Glory**" that I hope will help you to better understand holy portals of heaven.

Dear Friend,

May the glory of the Lord arise upon you and your family, in this hour when darkness has an itinerary to overcome. May your eyes of understanding be enlightened as the Light of God's glory illuminates every area and eternal avenue in this earth realm. May God in all of His glory overshadow you in the secret place that no foe can withstand. May you have supernatural knowledge of God in all of His glory, as He covers this earth with His very presence that all may see and believe. May His presence dwell with you everywhere your feet tread and give unto you His peace that surpasses all understanding. Be blessed my friend as you continue your journey.

Shalom,
Rebecca L. King

PORTALS

- All portals begin at the Throne of God and are opened by the authority of God as we take ownership of our divine position.

- Portals are supernatural openings in the heavenlies.

- Positioning yourself under an open portal brings forth unrecognizable revelation.

- Portals are shafts of eternity submerging into time.

- Portals are opened when people become desperate enough to be introduced to their destiny.

- Desolation comes forth when portals have been constricted; this becomes the abomination of desolation.

- Mantles come down through portals.

- When our spirit travels from eternity to earth, it travels through a portal.

- This same portal resides around us our whole lives here on this earth.

- It is up to us either to expand our portals or constrict them.

- Ways that expand our portals: Faith, Love, Forgiveness, Acceptance, Repentance, Renewal, Restoration, etc.

- Ways that constrict our portals: Fear, Doubt, Unbelief, Hate, Strife, Unforgiveness, Contentions, Rebellion, Confusions, Judgments, etc.

- A portal is a point of contact for heaven to invade earth.

- Your portal is the secret place.

- Every time that you tell a testimony it expands your portal.

- Portals open every time a child is born.

- Portals can be magnified.

- When your portals are expanded, they automatically break generational curses.

- Portals offer protection. A portal encapsulates Gods children. Shadrach, Meshach and Abednego were in a portal to protect them from the fire.

- Daniel was encapsulated in the lion's den by his portal.

- Desolation comes when a portal is constricted by man's fear.

- When portals are constricted, they can allow premature death.

- Obedience always brings forth an expansion to your portal. Disobedience will constrict your portal.

- Procrastination will constrict your portal.

- Portals have dominion over directions.

- Portals are ways to travel spiritually.

- Portals are the entrance to the city of heaven.

- Wisdom comes through your portal as you expand it by faith.

- The rod and staff that God speaks of are symbolic of portals of guidance and protection.

- Signs, wonders and miracles come through portals.

- When you expand your portal, you bring forth: more glory, more life and more love.

- Self-bitterness will constrict your portal.

- You decide by your faith how much of God's glory (light) travels through your portal.

- Promises come to pass through portals.

- The throne of grace is the entrance to your portal. When we are born, our spirit comes from God through our portal from His throne place of grace.

- Portals united with other portals bring forth the greater glory.

- Our inheritance is located within our portal.

- Revelation resides in your portal.

- Traumas cannot activate when a portal abounds.

- Peace is the center of your portal.

- Heavenly portals dominate demonic portals.

- There is a no time zone within your portal.

- Angels ascend and descend through portals.

- Portals are visible when expanded.

- Elijah and Moses appeared through their portals.

- Portals preserve you from persecution.

- Elijah went up in a whirlwind of glory through his portal.

OTHER BOOKS AVAILABLE BY REBECCA KING

THE WELL OF GOD'S GLORY UNVEILED

QUOTES BIRTHED OUT OF THE REVELATION OF GOD'S GLORY
VOLUME I

For more information concerning Harvest Time International Ministries and Rebecca L. King and to book speaking engagements contact us at:

Harvest Time International Ministries
108 W. Washington Ave.
Nashville, Georgia 31639
1.229.543.1080

Or visit our website at http://www.RebeccaKingMinistries.com

NOTES